THE BUSINESS WORDS YOU SHOULD KNOW

BRIAN TARCY

THE BUSINESS WORDS YOU SHOULD KNOW

BRIAN TARCY

1,500 Essential Words to Build the Vocabulary You Need for Business Today!

Adams Media Corporation
Holbrook, Massachusetts

Published by Adams Media Corporation
260 Center Street, Holbrook, MA 02343

ISBN: 1-55850-654-3

Printed in the United States of America.

J I H G F E D C B A

Library of Congress Cataloging-in-Publication Data
The business words you should know : 1,500 essential words to build the vocabulary
you need for business today! / Brian Tarcy.
p.   cm.
ISBN 1-55850-654-3 (pb)
1. Business—Dictionaries. 2. Commerce—Dictionaries. I. Title.
HF1001.T27   1996
650'.03—dc20   96–32579
CIP

This book is available at quantity discounts for bulk purchases.
For information, call 1-800-872-5627 (in Massachusetts, 617-767-8100).

Visit our home page at http://www.adamsmedia.com

Introduction

Whether you are an MBA or a new hire fresh out of school, you need to develop a broad vocabulary of business-related words and phrases in order to communicate effectively—and to understand the flood of crucial information you encounter every day. The business world is filled with specialized jargon and obscure and unusual terminology—from the worlds of finance, real estate, investing, and high-tech computers. *The Business Words You Should Know* will help you use the right word in every business situation. It includes over 1,500 of the most important terms and phrases, from demographics to distress prices, from jawboning to kangaroo bonds. Complete with easy-to-understand definitions and practical examples of the words in use, it is an invaluable reference that belongs on the desk of every business person.

A Note on Pronunciation

Pronunciation keys given in this book are rendered phonetically; no special symbols or systems have been employed.

It should be noted that many of the words in this book have secondary and tertiary pronunciations—not listed here for the sake of simplicity—that are entirely correct. Furthermore, regional influences often affect the pronunciations of certain words. What has been offered is the most common accepted means of pronouncing a given word, but by no means the only way.

abate (uh-BATE): To lower or mitigate. This term is used especially in relation to taxes.

> *The town will abate Harold's taxes because the assessor had overestimated the worth of his house.*

ABC Method (A-bee-see METH-ud): A way of keeping inventory that rates items by virtue of their dollar value. The most important ones, the expensive ones, deserve the most time and attention.

> *I want you to use the ABC Method . . . I want you to pay much more attention to software than you do to paper clips.*

abeyance (uh-BEY-ance): A state of temporary suspension. Used in law.

> *Sue knows her inheritance of the land is in abeyance until her great-uncle Waldo passes away.*

abrogate (AB-roe-gate): An official action that nullifies a previous official action. It is a repeal of a law, statute, order, treaty, or other official action.

> *City council studied the law about spitting on sidewalks after Crazy Earl asked them to start arresting people. City council didn't think it was worth the trouble, so it abrogated the outdated law.*

absorb the cost (ab-ZORB): When an unexpected cost of a project is not passed on to the customer, the cost is absorbed.

> *When tariffs went up, the car companies had to either raise their prices or absorb the cost of the tariffs.*

accelerated depreciation (ack-SELL-er-ate-ed dee-PRE-shee-a-shun): A way of calculating the rate of depreciation for a fixed asset. There are a number of methods that allow for bigger deductions in early years and smaller ones in later years.

> *Like all high technology, the new computer could be outdated within a year or two. Therefore, the company opted for accelerated depreciation on it.*

acceptable corporate behavior (ack-SEPT-a-bl KOR-po-rate be-HAYV-yur): Unwritten standards for corporate practices with other businesses and with society.

Cold-hearted downsizing is now considered acceptable corporate behavior, but a decade ago it would not have been.

accounting (uh-COUNT-ing): The system that keeps track of financial records for a person or company.

If you want to know about sales or profits, you should check with the accounting department.

accounting error (uh-COUNT-ing ER-ruhr): A mistake in calculation or measurement. Not fraud. An accounting error could be caused by two things: 1) misapplication of the Generally Accepted Accounting Principles (GAAP); or 2) negligence.

The reason our charitable write-offs came out wrong is because Jenkins made accounting errors on at least three of our charitable accounts.

accounting method (uh-COUNT-ing METH-ud): The formal way in which a business keeps its books. There are several ways to do various tasks, making numbers somewhat flexible from quarter to quarter.

When XYZ Company changed their accounting method, investors were leery of the new numbers.

accounting period (uh-COUNT-ing PEA-ree-uhd): The amount of time covered by an income statement. It is often a quarter, six months, or a year.

If you want to know about Bingo Company, it depends on the accounting period you examine. Bingo Company had huge overseas sales this last quarter, but earlier this year they didn't do as well because of their legal expenses.

accounting system (uh-COUNT-ing SIS-tem): The formal system includes the records, and information on where the data originated, as well as all employees and machines that handle accounting. Accounting systems in some industries, such as insurance, are regulated.

> *Before the consultant even looked at the troubled company's books, he wanted to know about the accounting system.*

accounts payable (uh-COUNTS PAY-a-bl): A list of debts owed by a business. Regular payments such as salaries and rent are not in this account. This account is for things such as services, inventory, and supplies.

> *The boss wanted to see a list of accounts payable so she would know what bills are due when.*

accounts receivable (uh-COUNTS ree-SEEV-a-bl): A list of what is owed to a company for its services or products.

> *Widgets Inc. didn't have a lot of cash on hand, but the leadership was not too worried since its accounts receivable was large.*

accrual accounting (uhk-KRU-al uh-COUNT-ing): This method acknowledges cash when earned and expenses when incurred. This method is not concerned with when bills are paid, but when they are sent or received.

> *Widgets Inc. uses accrual accounting to keep up to date on where its money is coming from and where it is going.*

accrued revenue (uhk-KRUED REV-eh-nue): Money that has been earned but hasn't yet been paid.

> *As soon as Jennifer finished the project, her company put the amount due under accrued revenue.*

acid test (a-SID test): The toughest test you can put a product or policy through. Acid is used to test metals. Acid corrodes other metals but it does not corrode gold. Passing an acid test is a sign of resilience and success.

Before the new software is sent to market, the engineers give one more try to make it do something wrong. "We'd rather the acid test be in the lab, not the market," said the chief engineer.

acquisition (ak-kweh-ZISH-uhn): The takeover of one company by another company.

Widgets Inc. wanted to increase revenues. That is the reason for the acquisition of Stuff Company.

acquisition cost (ak-kweh-ZISH-uhn cost): The price and fees associated with purchasing an item.

Management at Widgets Inc. decided not to buy new equipment because they couldn't afford the acquisition cost.

across the board (a-CROSS the bord): Includes everybody and everything in a certain group.

Workers in the plant were happy when management approved across-the-board pay hikes.

acts of God (acts uhv God): Disastrous natural occurrences beyond human control.

Our insurance policy covers the company from acts of God such as last week's hurricane.

actual cost (AK-chu-al cost): The price you paid to buy or produce an item. Not what it is worth. What you paid. The actual cost includes what you pay for storage and delivery.

The actual cost of the new machinery was less than what was originally quoted because we received a discount.

actuary (AK-chu-air-re): A mathematical official who calculates statistics about risks and premiums for insurance companies.

The new rates of car thefts in the city would have to be reported to the actuary.

add-on interest (ad-on IN-ter-est): Interest that is added to the principal of a loan.

Be sure to find out if your loan has add-on interest, because that will make it much more expensive.

adequate disclosure (AD-e-quate dis-CLO-zhur): Full truth in financial statements. Adequate disclosure is required so that readers of a financial statement can make the right investment or credit decisions.

We need to get the most recent sales numbers so we will have adequate disclosure on our loan application.

adjunct account (AD-junkt uh-COUNT): An account that accumulates the changes that occur to another account.

When the payment comes in, it will go right into the adjunct account so the balance on this account will not change.

adjustable-rate mortgage (ad-JUST-a-bl rate MOR-gihj): A mortgage having an interest rate that is periodically adjusted throughout the span of the loan. Rates can go up or down.

When you take out an adjustable-rate mortgage, you are rolling the dice that the economy will get stronger and rates will go down.

adjusted basis (ad-JUST-ed BAY-ses): Value as affected by depreciation or appreciation. What's it worth now?

If you look at the adjusted basis, you will know how much it depreciated since you purchased it.

adjuster (ad-JUST-er): Employee of insurance company whose job it is to settle claims, by examining the merits of all claims.

We have to wait to hear from the adjuster before we know how much we will receive for the damaged vehicle.

administration (ad-min-is-TRAY-shun): Management. Administration refers to the forces that run a company and perform its basic office services, not any one segment.

If you want to know why the checks are late, you are going to have to talk to someone in administration.

advance (ad-VANCE): Payment up front for goods or services.

As soon as I signed a contract, the company paid me half the money as an advance. When I finish the project, I'll get the rest.

advertise (AD-ver-tize): A paid form of communication that tries to call the public's attention to a company's product, service, or sale.

If you want people to know about your product, it helps a lot to advertise.

aerospace (A-er-o-space): The industry that includes airplanes, rockets, and other craft designed for air travel.

Because of the government's cuts in military spending, the aerospace industry was forced to downsize.

affirmative action (af-FIRM-a-tiv AK-chun): Policy to take steps to make up for previous discrimination. Often it means favoring minority job applicants over white ones.

The company had a poor history of hiring minorities until it started a program of affirmative action.

AFL-CIO, American Federation of Labor and Congress of Industrial Organizations (A-F-L C-I-O): Largest union in the United States.

> *The AFL-CIO is pushing hard to get an increase in the minimum wage.*

aggregate (AG-greh-gate): The sum of the parts.

> *The man in the corner office is examining the service contract so he wants to know the aggregate cost of repairs this year.*

aging of accounts (AJE-ing uhv uh-COUNTS): A way of classifying accounts by the time that has passed since the day of billing or the due date.

> *If you age the accounts, you will see that not many of our customers are very late with their payments.*

airbill (AIR-bill): The documents that go with a package to be sent by an express package or letter service.

> *We need to get the number on that airbill so the company can trace the package.*

allowance (al-LOW-ance): A reduction in price, often in compensation for a previous matter.

> *Since Widgets Inc. messed up the previous order, it gave Stuff Company an allowance of $1,000 on the new order.*

ambiguity (am-bih-GYU-ih-te): An unclear statement in an insurance policy. If language is subject to interpretations, it can go to court.

> *Our claim was held up because of an ambiguity in our policy. It looks like it has to go to court.*

America Online (A-MER-ih-ka on-line): The biggest commercial online service. America Online (often referred to by the letters AOL) charges a monthly fee and offers its members easy access to many services.

John decided to join America Online because of its access to many business magazines.

amortize (uh-MOR-tize): To write off an expense over a fixed period of time. The amount written off is the same each year until the write-off is complete.

We need to decide whether to amortize the new computer system over three years or five years.

analyst (AN-uh-list): A person who studies charts, graphs, data, or information and offers opinions as to what it means and where the business should go.

As soon as we get the reports from the three analysts, we'll hold a meeting to discuss our next step.

annual percentage rate (AN-you-al pehr-CENT-ehj rate): The cost of credit that a consumer pays, often referred to as APR.

The boss told Mary to check out the annual percentage rate from both banks before deciding anything.

annual report (AN-you-al re-PORT): Formal evaluation of financial status that companies put out at the end of the year. These are often glossy publications with a note from the president, and full of photographs and hype. The meat of the report is required by the Securities and Exchange Commission (SEC) and includes income statement, balance sheet, and cash flow reports.

This year's annual report by Widgets was so fancy it must have cost a fortune to produce. Too bad the bottom line looks so bad.

annuity (an-NEW-ih-te): Payments from an investment that come in regular installments.

> *The annuity from that bond investment is a nice amount.*

antitrust laws (AN-ti-trust laws): Laws that outlaw monopolies.

> *Widgets Inc. cannot take over the few competitors it has or it will have a problem with antitrust laws.*

apparel (ap-PAR-EL): Clothing. Apparel is an industry.

> *Coats and Jackets Inc. is a huge apparel company.*

application (ap-plih-KA-shun): A computer term for what software does.

> *Sure, we can design all sorts of software. What applications do you need?*

appraisal (uh-PRAZE-al): A professional estimate of a property's value.

> *We hadn't realized what this property was worth until we got the appraisal. We were astonished.*

arbitrage (AHR-bih-trage): A financial transaction in which an asset is purchased in one market and simultaneously sold in another market for a higher price.

> *If you study the markets, you will find that arbitrage is a good way to make money.*

arbitrator (AHR-bih-tra-tor): An impartial person whose job it is to solve disputes between two parties. Both sides present their case to the arbitrator, who then makes a decision.

> *When the union made a demand for a wage increase and the company made a demand for a pay cut, the only way to avoid a strike was to call in an arbitrator.*

arm's-length transaction (arms length trans-AK-chun): A transaction between two parties that are not related and are acting in their own self-interest.

> *When Widgets Inc. sold 5,000 widgets to Stuff Company, it was an arm's-length transaction, but when Widgets Inc. sold 5,000 widgets to its subsidiary, it was not.*

arrears (ar-REARS): A debt that has not been paid on time.

> *The rent on the building is in arrears, so the landlord is threatening to throw us out.*

ASCII (ASK-ee): American Standard Code for Information Interchange. This is the standard code for representing text.

> *You have to convert the story into ASCII before sending it to the magazine, then they can read it and convert it into their software.*

Automated Teller Machine, also known as ATM (AW-toe-mate-ed TELL-er ma-SHEEN): A computerized terminal that allows people to access their bank accounts for deposits or withdrawals with the use of an ATM card and an individual code.

> *Even though the bank is closed, we can still get some cash at the automated teller machine.*

audit (AW-dit): Inspection of accounting records to verify the accuracy of them.

> *The recent audit revealed some problems in the recordkeeping at Widgets Inc.*

audit cycle (Aw-dit SI-kl): Recurring period of time that an accountant conducts an audit.

> *The audit cycle for inventory has inventory being audited every six months—in November and May.*

average age of inventory (AV-er-ehg age of in-ven-toh-re): How long, in terms of days, it takes to sell an average inventory item.

The average age of inventory for that particular line of widgets has dropped from 123 days to 86 days because of the sale we had last month.

Baby Bell (BA-be bell): A regional telephone company created by the breakup of AT&T. The name is a takeoff of the nickname for AT&T, Ma Bell.

The long-distance rates of the Baby Bell are lower than those of its smaller competitors.

back-end load (bak end load): A commission charged for a mutual fund that must be paid when the mutual fund is sold.

He didn't want to sell the mutual fund for two reasons: it has not done well and it has a back-end load.

back order (bak OR-dehr): When there is not enough inventory to fill a customer's order, it is considered on back order.

Those widgets have been on back order for three months. It is time to cancel that order and try and find them at some other company.

backslash (BAK-slash): This is a backslash (\). It is different from a regular slash (/). It is not found on a typewriter keyboard, only on a computer keyboard, and is used in computer commands.

If you forget to put the backslash in, the computer will misread your command.

backup (bak up): Can be used as a noun or a verb. Either a copy of a computer file, or to make a copy of a computer file.

It's a good thing we have a backup of that file. Or . . . Be sure to backup that file.

backward vertical integration (BAK-ward VER-tih-cal in-teh-gra-shun): A way to eliminate middlemen. With backward vertical integration, a company takes control of its supplies, thus cutting costs and streamlining operations.

Our suppliers keep raising their prices so much that I think we should consider backward vertical integration.

bad debt (bad det): An uncollectable debt.

With the economic downturn, Widgets Inc. found itself with a lot of bad debt because so many of its customers went bankrupt.

bail bond (BA-ehl bond): A guarantee of money that a prisoner released from jail will be present in court when required.

The company had to post a big bail bond to get the CEO out of jail.

bait and switch (bate and switch): An illegal way to deceive consumers by advertising one item at a low price but not having it in stock, and then trying to sell the consumer a much pricier item.

We went to the store for the $200 television that was advertised, but it was just a bait and switch. They were out of that television, but tried to sell us a $500 one instead.

balance (BAL-ahns): The amount in an account. The bottom line. The difference between debits and credits.

Before you spend any money from that account, be sure to check the balance to see how much you have to spend.

balanced budget (BAL-ahnst BUDJ-et): A budget in which no more is spent than is taken in. This has become an issue in politics because the federal government has not had a balanced budget in decades.

Without a balanced budget, services we use now will still be being paid for by generations in the future.

balance of trade (BAL-ahns of trade): A country's difference between exports and imports over a given period of time.

The new products by Widgets Inc. were so popular overseas that they helped the balance of trade because so many more widgets were going out of the country than were being imported.

balance sheet (BAL-ahns sheet): A financial statement showing debits and credits for a company after a specific period.

When the president of Widgets Inc. looked at the balance sheet, he realized the company was losing money and had to make some drastic changes.

balloon payment (bal-LOON PAY-ment): A final payment on a loan that pays it off before it is due. A balloon payment is larger than a regular payment.

They wanted to end the burden of the debt so they finished it off with a balloon payment.

bankruptcy (BANK-rupt-see): A legal inability to pay debts.

When Widgets Inc. lost three big contracts, it had so many debts it had no choice but to file for bankruptcy.

bar code (bar code): A series of wide and narrow lines and numbers that are on many products. Computers scan these codes and read product information into cash registers.

During the 1992 election, President Bush was amazed at how bar codes worked.

bargain purchase (BAR-gihn PUR-chess): Something that is bought for less than fair market value.

The furniture you bought at the auction was a bargain purchase. If you had gone to a furniture store, it would have cost twice as much.

barometer (ba-ROM-eh-ter): A measuring device.

Profits are a good barometer of success.

barriers to entry (BAR-re-ers to EN-tre): Conditions that make it difficult to start a new business in a certain industry.

Learning the high technology of widgets is a definite barrier to entry in that business.

barter (BAR-ter): When two companies trade goods or services without using money.

Widgets Inc. and Stuff Company have a barter agreement in which three widgets are traded for every one piece of stuff.

base period (base PEH-re-ohd): A set period of time that is used as a standard for measuring economic data.

The base period for measuring widget sales is one year.

base-year analysis (bas year uh-NAL-ih-sis): A means of analyzing economic data by using one specific year as a measuring stick. This allows analysts to use "constant dollars" so they can see trends without the effect of inflation.

When the analyst did a base-year analysis, she saw that profits at Widgets Inc. were actually going down.

BASIC (BA-sik): This stands for Beginners All-purpose Symbolic Instruction Code. It is a computer programming language that is one of the easiest to understand.

You should be able to readjust that program. It is written in BASIC.

batch processing (bach PROSS-ess-ing): Computer processing which is done in sequential order that is inputted ahead of time.

The bills were sent out by a batch processing program.

baud (bawd): The speed at which a computer modem sends or receives data. A baud rate refers to the bits per second that are transferred over a phone line.

> *If your modem has a fast baud rate, you will receive data faster and you will cut your phone costs.*

beached whale (beached whale): A company that apppears on the verge of death. Taken from the mysterious tendency of some whales to beach themselves and then die.

> *Widgets Inc. was a beached whale until Joe Cooper took over and restructured the entire company. Amazingly, the company came back to life and is now quite healthy.*

bean counter (bean COUN-ter): A derogatory, sarcastic term used for accountants who keep track of every little item without regard for the big picture.

> *My biggest complaint about this company is that you can't make a decision around here without consulting the bean counters.*

bear market (bear MAHR-ket): A long period of falling prices. The opposite of a bull market.

> *The bear market has some investors worried that the country could be falling into a deep recession.*

bedroom community (BED-room cuhm-MU-nih-te): A suburb near a city from where it is presumed many people commute to work in the city.

> *Big City Heights is a bedroom community of Big City. There are not many jobs in Big City Heights but there are an awful lot of nice houses.*

behavioral accounting (be-HAYV-yur-al uh-COUNT-ing): An accounting approach that stresses the human side of decision making.

> *When you use behavioral accounting, managers will feel empowered and more a part of the decision making process.*

behavior modification (be-HAYV-yur mod-ih-fih-ka-shun): A way of changing the behavior of employees with positive or negative reinforcement.

> *The bonus plan is working well as behavior modification because everyone is working harder.*

bellwether (BELL-weth-er): An investment that is considered an indicator of the market's overall direction.

> *Widgets Inc. is such a huge company and has so many big investors that it is a bellwether of the market.*

benchmark (BENCH-mark): A unit that is used for comparison of quality or value.

> *Joe Talker's sales numbers were considered a benchmark for all the other salesmen at Widgets Inc.*

bid (bid): The amount offered by someone or some company to purchase something at an auction.

> *My bid was the highest, so I am now the proud owner of an antique widget.*

Big Six accounting firms (big six uh-COUNT-ing firms): The largest accounting firms in the country, which do the auditing and tax work for many of the country's biggest corporations. They are: Arthur Anderson & Co., Coopers & Lybrand, Deloitte & Touche, Ernst & Young, KPMG Peat Marwick, and Price Waterhouse & Co.

> *When my son graduates with his accounting degree, his dream is to go work for one of the Big Six.*

Big Steel (big steel): The big U.S. steel companies, such as USX Corporation, which was formerly known as U.S. Steel Corporation.

> *The automotive industry is less dependent on Big Steel and more dependent on foreign imports.*

big-ticket items (big TICK-et I-tems): Consumer purchases that cost a lot of money. These are often purchased with credit.

> *John Jones didn't want to get a big-screen television because he said his paycheck couldn't pay for another big-ticket item after the purchase of two new cars last year.*

bill of sale (bill of sale): A document that transfers ownership of goods.

> *Don't lose the bill of sale in case something goes wrong and you want to take it back.*

bit (bit): A binary digit. A bit can only be a 0 or a 1. In a computer, a bit is the smallest unit of memory.

> *It is amazing how many bits it takes to make even a small file.*

black market (black MAHR-ket): An unregulated market in which goods are sold illegally.

> *The only place that you can buy crack cocaine is on the black market.*

blanket insurance policy (BLAN-ket in-SHURE-ehns POL-ih-se): A single policy that covers different properties in different locations, or the same property in different locations, or different property in the same location. It is ideal for a chain store.

> *When Widgets Inc. opened factory outlets across the country, it took out a blanket insurance policy.*

bleed (bleed): To take more money from a project or person than is warranted, often at the expense of upkeep.

> *There was no upkeep on that property at all. The landlord was just bleeding the project.*

blind trust (blind trust): A trust in which the assets are not disclosed to the owner so the owner, often in a position of public authority, cannot be accused of making decisions for personal benefit.

> *When Sue Talker decided to run for mayor, she had all of her assets placed into a blind trust.*

bloated company (BLOAT-ed COHM-pah-ne): A large company that is slow on its feet, full of bureaucracy, and unable to make quick changes.

> *The years of success at Widgets Inc. brought about a complacency that caused many analysts to peg it as a bloated company.*

blowout (BLO-out): A quick sale of retail items at reduced prices. This is a method of reducing inventory.

> *Zebra Motors is having a weekend blowout sale before the new models come in next week.*

blue chip (blue chip): Common stock of a national company that has a long record of growth and is expected to continue to grow.

> *Alfred Moneybags III learned from his grandfather to only invest in blue chip stocks like Widgets Inc., which has been the largest manufacturer of widgets for the past century.*

blue collar (blue COL-lahr): A worker who works with his hands.

> *When Sam Hammer went to college, it was clear to his father, who works in the Widget factory, that Sam would be the first of the Hammer family men who would not have a blue-collar job. Sam wants to be a stockbroker.*

blueprint (BLU-print): A photographic reproduction of architecture or engineering plans. The reproduction is in white, on a blue background . . . A blueprint is also a general term for a plan of action.

> *We have to have the blueprint for the new factory ready for tomorrow night's planning commission meeting. Or . . . The blueprint for success is hard work mixed with luck.*

board of directors (bord of dih-RECT-ors): This is the group that elects operating officers and the chief executive for a company. The members of the board of directors, who meet several times a year and are paid, are elected by stockholders.

> *The board of directors were so upset by the performance of the company's stock that they fired the CEO and launched a nationwide search for someone to turn the company around.*

boardroom (BORD-room): Fancy room where the company's board of directors meets.

> *Frank Goof was in trouble for taking his coffee break in the boardroom rather than the employee lunchroom.*

body language (BOD-e LAN-gwahj): Unintended, nonverbal communication that some say reveals more about a person's true intent than their verbal communication.

> *Mary Eloquent attributed her success in sales to her ability to read her potential customers' body language.*

boilerplate (BOIL-er-plate): Standardized language in a preprinted agreement.

> *Now that we have an handshake agreement, we'll get you a boilerplate that we've used in many similiar agreements.*

bond (bond): A loan certificate given by a government or corporation that has a fixed maturity date and a fixed interest rate. This is a common way to raise money.

> *The town floated a bond to pay for the new sewer system.*

book value (book VAL-u): Gross value minus depreciation. Book value can be more or less than market value. It is an estimate to give an idea of what the market value may be.

> *The book value of our old computer system is lower than what we think it could be worth if we sold it to a startup company.*

boom (boom): A prolonged period of rising prices. The opposite of a bust.

> *The stock market boom has been good for everyone who has money invested.*

boom-and-bust cycle (boom and bust SI-kl): The pattern of a market going up and then down.

> *If you are smart, you can read the boom-and-bust cycle and buy before the boom and then sell before the market goes bust.*

boondoggle (BOON-dog-gl): A worthless, unneccessary project that is done simply to create work.

> *The idea of trying to make edible widgets was a boondoggle from its start. The only reason for attempting it was because Mr. Harebrain always wanted to be in the food business.*

boot (boot): The term for starting a computer.

> *No wonder there is nothing on the screen. You haven't even booted up the system yet.*

bootstrap acquisition (BOOT-strap ak-kweh-ZISH-uhn): Financing an acquisition with a company's excess cash.

> *The management of Widgets Inc. was so confident that acquiring Stuff Company was a good idea that, despite difficulty in getting financing, they went ahead with a bootstrap acquisition.*

borrow (BOR-ro): To request and then take from another with the promise to pay back that amount plus interest.

> *In order to upgrade the machinery, Widgets Inc. had to borrow $4 million.*

bottom line (BOT-tohm line): Net profit or loss on a project, or for a specific period of time.

> *When Wilma Warbucks saw the bottom line on the European project, she was ecstatic because the profits were larger than she had ever imagined.*

boycott (BOY-kot): A concerted effort by a group of people to refuse to buy a certain product. This gives those people leverage to force a company to change some unpopular policy or to make changes to a dangerous or unpopular product.

> *Environmentalists were leading a boycott of products by Widgets Inc. to force the company to quit polluting Lake Water.*

bracket creep (BRACK-et creep): This happens when you make more money and find yourself in a higher tax bracket.

> *When Sue Ambition received her pay raise, she hadn't realized she would be facing bracket creep causing her to pay a higher percentage of her income in taxes.*

brainstorming (BRAIN-storm-ing): A process where a number of people sit together throwing out ideas to one another and feeding off one another's ideas to come up with a solution to a business problem.

> *For the new marketing plan, the president called for a daylong brainstorming session.*

brand association (brand as-so-se-A-shun): When a brand becomes known as the product category.

> *When Frank asked for a Xerox of his report, he made a brand association because he didn't necessarily want his copies from a Xerox machine. He merely wanted his report photocopied.*

brand loyalty (brand LOY-al-te): When a consumer becomes convinced that a particular brand of a product is the best for them, they have brand loyalty. All companies want their customers to develop brand loyalty because that means they become repeat customers.

Despite the fact that many companies make gizmos, Harry always bought Widget gizmos because of his brand loyalty.

brand manager (brand MAN-ah-jur): The person resonsible for how a particular brand is marketed. A company that sells many different brands has brand managers to ensure that each brand is given the proper attention.

Sheila Spitfire became brand manager of the doohickey brand of widgets and launched a nationwide advertising campaign to differentiate doohickeys from other, less expensive, widgets.

brand marketing (brand MAHR-ket-ing): How a particular brand is marketed.

The brand marketing of Doohickeys was brilliant because it made consumers think of that brand as a status symbol.

breach (breech): Nonfulfillment of an agreement.

When Ralph Rolodex quit his job without finishing the project he was hired for, it was a breach of contract.

bridge loan (brij loan): A short-term loan given in anticipation of long-term financing.

The bank offered us a bridge loan to get started on the project while the paperwork is being finished for the 30-year loan.

broker (BRO-ker): A person who gets buyers and sellers together and helps them do business.

If you want to sell your stock in Widgets Inc., you should contact your broker.

brokerage (BRO-ker-ehj): A broker is in the brokerage business... Or... A brokerage is the amount paid to a broker for his work on a deal.

> *Did you see that Reginald opened up his own brokerage business? Or... Reginald received a $3,000 brokerage on that $50,000 deal.*

browser (BROWS-er): An Internet search engine that will search the World Wide Web for sites that match whatever it is you type. If you type "dog," a browser will find all the sites it can that mention "dog." Some browsers search titles, some search the entire site. Not every web site is found by every browser.

> *Jim was doing a school project about volcanoes. When he typed the word into his browser, it found 578 Web sites on volcanoes.*

budget (BUJ-et): A plan of how much money is expected to come in and how much money is expected to be spent for a given period. A budget is specific about what things money will be spent on and how much is available to spend.

> *Our budget for expenses this year only pays for salaries. We are not budgeted to buy any new equipment.*

bug (bug): When something goes wrong on a computer program, it is said to have a bug. A bug is an error in the program.

> *We asked for our money back from Smartypants Software because their accounting software had a bug in it that caused us to overpay everyone last week.*

bull market (bull MAHR-ket): A long period of rising prices. The opposite of a bear market.

> *The bull market of the past two years has made some people very rich, but many say it can't last forever.*

burnout (BURN-out): When someone loses energy and enthusiasm for a job they once loved, they have burnout.

Nancy used to be the best teacher, but she's been dealing with adolescents for so long that she now has burnout and she's just doing it for the paycheck.

business cycle (BIZ-ness SI-kl): The general pattern of the economy from periods of recession to growth and back, etc.

Don't sell your property during this bad part of the business cycle. I recommend waiting until the economy gets good again.

business day (BIZ-ness day): The conventional business day is 9 A.M. to 5 P.M. Business days are Monday through Friday.

On Friday, Jenny was told to get the report to her boss by the end of the next business day. She knew that meant she had until 5 P.M. on Monday.

business-to-business advertising (BIZness to BIZ-ness AD-ver-tize-ing): This is a specific type of advertising aimed at business people. Its purpose is to sell products or services for use by businesses. This type of advertising often uses trade publications.

It is more efficient to use business-to-business advertising to try to sell parts for widget-making machines than it is to do broad, consumer advertising. That's why we advertise in Widgetworld *magazine.*

business service (BIZ-ness SERV-iss): Something that is performed for a business. A service includes consulting, accounting, advertising, sales, etc.

Not only has our cost of supplies gone up, but so has our cost of business services.

bust (bust): A prolonged period of falling prices. The opposite of a boom.

After the election of the protectionist president, the market went bust.

buy-back agreement (BI-back uh-GREE-ment): A clause in a sales agreement that requires the seller to repurchase property if a certain event occurs within a given period of time.

When Stephanie Ladderclimber was transferred three months after she purchased a house, she was not worried about having to sell it because she had a buy-back agreement with the person who sold it to her.

buzzword (BUZZ-werd): New, slang word used by a group in a specific industry that has meaning to the group, but is obscure to others.

I've never worked in the widget industry before so I don't understand all the buzzwords.

by-product (BI PROD-ukt): An incidental product that is produced in the process of making something else.

In the lumber business, one by-product is sawdust.

by the book (by the book): Inflexible adherence to a strict set of written procedures.

Everything at Widgets Inc. is done by the book. Employees may as well freeze their brains when they are at work since they are not allowed to think for themselves.

byte (bite): A computer term. A byte is equal to eight bits of memory.

I need to know how many bytes of memory that program uses.

calendar year (KAL-en-der year): The time from January 1 to December 31. A calendar year is different from a fiscal year.

Our sales for the last calendar year were great.

call option (kall OP-shun): The right to buy a specific number of shares of stock by a deadline.

I have a call option on Widget Inc. stock.

capacity (ka-PASS-ih-te): The most that a company can produce.

When we bought our new machinery, we raised our capacity quite a bit.

capital gain (KAP-ih-tel gain): The amount of money made after selling something for more than it was bought.

We bought the house for $100,000 and sold it for $150,000. The capital gain was $50,000.

capital projects fund (KAP-ih-tel PROJ-ekts fund): A governmental accounting fund for the purpose of acquisition or construction of large projects.

When the town of Widgetville Heights needed a new elementary school, officials raised taxes to raise money for the capital projects fund.

capital structure (KAP-ih-tel STRUK-chure): The equity of an owner in stock. Capital structure includes common stock and preferred stock. Some say it includes long-term debt, since that is used to finance long-term assets. Not all agree.

My accountant wanted to know if I was diversified enough, so he is studying my capital structure.

carrier (KAR-re-er): A business that sells transportion.

The trucking company we use, Dependable Drivers Company, is reasonably priced and very efficient. Who is your carrier?

carrot and stick (KAR-rut and stik): A negotiating strategy of offering enticements to accept a deal and reprisals if the other side does not.

> *Management offered the union big raises to come back to the dangerous factory; however, management said if the strike continued it would hire replacement workers. That was a carrot and stick approach to negotiations.*

carte blanche (kart blanch): The freedom to act as one sees fit. Carte blanche is a blank check.

> *When Andy Danife was hired as sales manager, he was given carte blanche over the department. Two weeks later, he fired everybody and hired an entirely new staff.*

case study (kase STUD-e): The study of a specific business situation for the purpose of learning how decisions are made and how to make better decisions.

> *If you look at these two case studies of how two companies tried unsuccessfully to compete in the widget industry, you will see the flexibility that Widgets Inc. has for dealing with competition. Taken together, these two are classic examples of a company being quick on its feet.*

cash (kash): Cash is money that has immediate value. It does not include postdated checks, or IOUs.

> *After I deposited my check, I had $4,328 of cash in my account.*

cash cow (kash kow): When a business or product continuously makes a lot of money, it is a cash cow.

> *Boxing writers (and business writers) say that Mike Tyson is a cash cow for his promotor, Don King. For his last fight, Tyson received $30 million. He'll probably get double that amount for his next fight. Of course, King gets a healthy percentage of anything Tyson earns.*

cash flow (kash flo): The net amount of cash that goes in or out. Positive cash flow means you have more money coming in than going out. Negative cash flow means more is going out than coming in.

> *Widgets Inc. could not make any big capital investments because its cash flow situation was not good.*

cash on delivery (COD) (cash on de-LIV-er-e): A method of delivery that requires cash or a certified check payment when the product is delivered. Collect on delivery uses the same initials (COD) and means the same thing.

> *Wally ordered his new software COD, so he was sure to go to the bank and get a certified check for $300.*

catastrophe policy (ka-TAS-tro-fe POL-ih-se): A major medical insurance policy that will cover large medical expenses.

> *If Wanda hadn't had a catastrophe policy, she would have lost her house after her open heart surgery.*

caveat emptor (KAH-ve-at EMP-tor): "Let the buyer beware," in Latin.

> *When I complained to the salesman that the car he sold me was a lemon, he just snickered and said, "Caveat emptor."*

CD-ROM (c d rom): This stands for Compact Disk Read-Only Memory. A CD-ROM is a compact disk much like an audio disk, but the information is read into a computer medium.

> *Pete Procrastinate needed to do his research project overnight. Luckily, he had an entire set of encyclopedias on a CD-ROM.*

Central Processing Unit (CPU) (SEN-tral PROSS-ess-ing U-nit): The part of a computer that does all the main calculations.

> *I want to get a new computer because I need a more powerful CPU to run the new software on the market.*

certificate (ser-TIF-ih-cate): A fancy document that has all the printed information about what it represents.

Esther liked to look at her stock certificates because they were such nice documents, and because they reminded her of how much stock she had in Widgets Inc.

Certificate of Deposit (CD) (ser-TIF-ih-cate of de-POS-it): If an investment instrument in which an investor deposits a set amount for a set period of time and receives a fixed rate of return. The investor cannot withraw funds early without a penalty.

Nick Norisk put his money into certificates of deposit. He had one one-year CD, one five-year CD, and one ten-year CD.

certified check (SER-tih-fied chek): A check that a bank guarantees will be paid.

The phone company wants a certified check by Friday or your phone will be turned off.

Certified Financial Planner (CFP) (SER-tih-fied fi-NAN-shel PLAN-ner): A licensed professional who has passed tests in many areas of finance including insurance, investments, employee-benefit plans, estate planning, and taxation. These professionals develop personalized financial plans for their clients.

When Patty Party turned thirty years old, she realized she had less than $1,000 in the bank. That was when she decided she would benefit from seeing a personal financial planner.

Certified Public Accountant (CPA) (SER-tih-fied PUB-lik uh-COUNT-ent): An accountant who has passed a stringent test and has the proper experience as required by the particular state where the accountant works.

Robert Numberman was always good at math but he was amazed at how difficult it was to become a CPA.

chain of command (chain of cum-MAND): The structure in which orders are given in an organization.

> *John is Jane's boss. Jane is Frank's boss. Frank is Fred's boss. Fred is Sue's boss. Sue is Tom's boss. When Tom wants John to know anything, he must go through the chain of command.*

chairman of the board (CHAIR-man of the bord): The highest-ranking officer in a corporation. A board member who presides over the meetings of the board.

> *The chairman of the board didn't like the advertising strategy, so he led the meeting in the direction of making a change. By the end, the board ordered the CEO to study what advertising options would be best.*

Chapter 7 of the 1978 Bankruptcy Act (BANK-rupt-see): When a business files for Chapter 7 Bankruptcy, a court-appointed trustee takes over the business. The entire goal is to avoid further losses. Sometimes, it means liquidation. Sometimes it means continuing to operate with a change in management.

> *Almostwidgets Company filed for Chapter 7 Bankruptcy. The inventory was sold, and the owners began working on their resumes.*

Chapter 11 of the 1978 Bankruptcy Act (BANK-rupt-see): Reorganization of a company in order to try to make a new start. The company stays in possession of the owners.

> *Widget Nation filed for Chapter 11 Bankruptcy so it could reorganize and concentrate on a specific niche of the market.*

chat (chat): Holding a conversation on a computer with others. You can talk to a group of people, or to an individual. Chat groups are often organized around a subject. You "say" what you want by typing, and you "listen" by reading what others have typed.

> *When I go into a chat group, I meet people from all over the world. My favorite is the chat group about music.*

Chief Executive Officer (CEO) (c e o): The boss. The person who can honestly say, "The buck stops here." The CEO reports only to the board of directors.

> *Everyone at Widgets Inc. has been nervous since the CEO announced he would soon eliminate 25 percent of all jobs.*

Chief Financial Officer (CFO) (c f o): Corporate officer who has authority to make financial decisions and to authorize expenses.

> *Before Walter even began examining the new accounting software on the market, he went to see the CFO to be sure the company would approve the expenditure. He justified it to the CFO by saying it would improve efficiency.*

Chief Operating Officer (COO) (c o o): The person directly in charge of the day-to-day operations of a company.

> *When the production line broke down, the production manager had to explain why it happened to the COO, who was not the least bit happy.*

child and dependent care credit (child and de-PEND-ent care KRED-it): A tax credit for taking care of dependents.

> *When Jim's wife became pregnant in January, he knew that he would get a child and dependent care credit for this year.*

chip (chip): A semiconductor body that holds an integrated circuit.

> *The increased popularity of computers has made this a good time to be in the chip business.*

civil damages (SIV-ihl DAM-ehj-ez): The money a winning plaintiff is due from a losing plaintiff in a court of law.

> *The faulty gas tank on the new model by Cheepcar Motors has lawyers worried about civil damages.*

claim (klaim): A request by an insured for compensation from an insurance company to cover loss from a risk that was insured.

The chemical facility for Widgets Inc. burned to the ground in a fire. The company has filed a claim with its insurance company. Widgets Inc. hopes the claim is settled soon because it has already started building a new chemical facility, and the claim could cover the cost of construction and equipment.

claim report (klaim re-PORT): A claim report is issued by an adjuster to an insurance company. The report interprets the policy and the damage and tells the amount the company is obligated to pay for the loss.

Fred didn't know how much he would receive for his damaged truck. His insurance agent told him, "We'll have to wait until we see the claim report."

clean hands (kleen hands): Ethical behavior. If a person follows the law and common morals, that person is said to have clean hands.

"They can investigate all they want," said Holden, laughing. "They won't find anything on me. My hands are clean."

clear (klear): In banking, a check is clear when funds have been paid to the holder of a check. In finance, the profit is the amount cleared.

I cannot pay my bills until the check I received for the big freelance project has cleared. Or . . . For that project, after expenses, I cleared $50,000.

client (KLI-ent): The customer of a professional services company.

The president of the advertising company told his staff that the client was not happy with the new campaign, and may look for a new agency.

client/server technology (KLI-ent SERV-er): Computer technology that allows a personal computer to connect to a larger computer, utilizing the power of both.

> *"Going into client/server is the wave of the future," said the president of Smartypants Software.*

clone (klone): A nearly exact duplicate of an IBM computer. A clone can run all software that was designed to run on an IBM computer.

> *I want to get an IBM clone because I have a lot of software from my old IBM that I need to be able to use.*

closed shop (klozed shop): A company in which workers are required to join a union before they are allowed to work there.

> *I tried to get a job in the Widgets factory but first I had to join the International Brotherhood of Widget Workers because Widgets Inc. is a closed shop.*

closing (Kloze-ing): The completion of a real estate deal. A closing usually involves payment of some portion of the purchase price, and delivery of the deed.

> *We are so excited that we are finally going to own a house. Our closing is two weeks from today.*

closing costs (KLOZE-ing kosts): The fees and expenses due on the closing date by the buyer and seller in a real estate transaction. Closing costs include brokerage commission, inspection and appraisal fees, lender discount points, and attorney's fees.

> *We can't wait to move into the new house, but we won't be able to afford any new furniture. The closing costs were really high.*

cluster zoning (KLUS-ter ZONE-ing): Zoning for subdivisons in which houses are put close together and surrounded by open space shared by all. This is different from regular zoning in which houses are equally spaced and each house lot has a greater amount of space. The open space in a cluster development is shared by all the residents.

I like the idea of moving into a development where there is cluster zoning because I will be closer to my neighbors, and my kids will have more room to play.

cold call (kold kall): A sales call, either in person or by phone, that the potential customer is not expecting.

When you do a cold call, you are lucky if the person will even listen to your sales pitch.

collaborative work (kul-LAB-o-rah-tiv werk): When two or more individuals or companies work together on a project, it is collaborative work.

The new book by the movie star, Joe Charisma, is a collaborative work of Charisma and his ghostwriter, William Novak.

collateral (kuhl-LAT-er-el): An asset a borrower puts forth as a guarantee that a loan will be repaid.

When John started his company, Widget Renovations, he put his house up as collateral for the startup loan.

collateralized mortgage obligations (kuhl-LAT-er-el-ized MOR-gej ob-lih-GA-shuns): A bond that is backed by mortgage pools.

Sue decided to invest in collateralized mortgage obligations because she saw them as a way to make some good money.

commingled trust fund (kum-MIN-gld trust fund): When two or more pension funds are managed under a common portfolio, they are a commingled trust fund.

Our pension is in a huge commingled trust that we assume is quite safe.

commodity (kum-MOD-ih-te): Something that exists in the physical world and is bought and sold.

A commodity that is sold in Idaho is potatoes.

common area (KOM-mun a-RE-ah): Area of a property that is available for use by all owners or tenants.

John didn't like some of the other tenants in his condominium complex using the swimming pool when he did. But he knew that the pool was a common area and everybody had a right to use it.

common stock (KOM-mun stok): Stock that offers the greatest potential risk and reward. An investor who owns common stock benefits the most if a company is going good, and loses the most if a company is going bad. Owners of common stock elect the board of directors.

Sheila heard that Widgets Inc. was coming out with a hot new product so she bought a bunch of common stock, expecting to make a good profit. When the product turned out to be flawed, she found her stock had plummeted in price.

common stock equivalent (KOM-MUN stok e-KWIV-ah-lent): A security that has provisions allowing it to be converted into common stock.

When John heard about the new product being put out by Widgets Inc., he was glad that he had a common stock equivalent in the company.

comparable worth (KOM-pah-rah-bl werth): A theory of employment that says employees should be paid based on their worth to the company, not based on other factors such as age or sex.

Monica believed that if her company based her pay on comparable worth, she would probably double her salary. However, since she was in a company dominated by males, she knew that wouldn't happen any time soon.

comparison shopping (KUM-pa-rih-sun SHOP-ing): A method of shopping in which a consumer researches a particular product by surveying a number of stores as well as advertisements. The idea is to find the best product for the best price.

Before Ralph spent more than $30,000 for his new car, he did some comparison shopping at a number of dealers in the area. When he found the best price, he decided to buy.

competition (kom-peh-TISH-un): A rivalry between companies and products in the marketplace.

Before you start a business, it is essential to study the competition.

compliance audit (kum-PLI-ens AW-dit): An audit of contractual agreements, ensuring there has been compliance on things such as loan agreements and regulatory requirements.

Before we move into the second phase of the contract, we have to wait for a compliance audit of the first phase.

component (kum-PO-nent): A part of a whole system.

A hard drive is just one component of my new computer.

compound interest (COM-pound IN-ter-est): Interest that is earned on a principal plus previous interest. If an investment of $1,000 earns $100 in the first year, the interest rate of 10 percent will apply to the full $1,100 the second year.

After Sam received his inheritance, he wanted to find a bank account that received compound interest because he knew his money would grow fast in such an account.

comprehensive general liability insurance (com-PRE-hen-siv jen-er-ul li-ah-BIL-ih-te in-SHURE-ens): An all-encompassing insurance policy for a company that covers all risks that are not specifically excluded.

Widgets Inc. found it received a better deal and an easier to understand policy when it took out comprehensive general liability insurance rather than look for many policies covering many things.

Compuserve (COMP-u-serv): One of the big commercial online services.

There are a number of business publications on Compuserve that I really like.

computer assisted design (CAD) (kum-PUTE-er as-SIST-ed de-ZINE): A type of computer program for architects and engineers that allows them to try their ideas in simulated three-dimensional conditions. The program can do all mathematical equations on the strength and flexibility of a structure while also simulating weather as well as natural and man-made disasters.

"Nowadays, every architect is an expert with CAD," said Johnson, who was retiring from the firm.

computer assisted transcription (CAT) (kum-PUTE-er as-SIST-ed trans-SKRIP-shun): The copying of the contents of an audio tape into a computer for storage and retrieval.

We don't have to have a secretary at our meetings to take minutes. We can use CAT.

concept test (KON-sept test): When an advertising concept has been developed but not yet implemented, there is often a test of its effectiveness before a small group.

The concept test for the slogan "A widget the whole family can value," showed that not many people were interested in such a widget.

condominium (kon-do-MIN-e-um): A form of property ownership in which the owner owns the house or apartment, but the outside is part of a common area that is maintained by a management company. All condominium owners must pay a maintenance fee.

Cindy liked owning her condominium better than renting, but her dream was to buy a house so she could have her own yard and garden.

Conference Board, The (KON-fer-ens bord): A nonprofit group that studies business management and economic issues and then publishes recommendations.

> *The Conference Board issued a paper about the use of contingent workers that was very interesting.*

conference call (KON-fer-ens kall): A telephone connection that allows three or more people to talk to one another.

> *The schedules of the board of directors didn't coincide for an in-house meeting for two months. But for the emergency this week, they met on a conference call.*

conglomerate (kon-GLOM-er-ate): When many different businesses are joined together in one corporation, that corporation is a conglomerate.

> *Widget Parts Company is not a small company, but rather part of the huge conglomerate, Widgets Inc., which even has a cereal company and a tire company under its umbrella.*

consequential loss (kon-se-KWEN-shul loss): A loss in income that results from a loss of property.

> *After the fire in the arena, the team ownership realized the consequential loss was huge. After all, the team used to play in a 17,000-seat arena, but would now have to play in the local college arena, which only has 3,000 seats. That's a consequential loss of 14,000 tickets that can't be sold for every game.*

consolidation (kun-sol-ih-DA-shun): The formation of a new corporation from two or more existing corporations.

> *Widgets Inc. was formed many years ago after the consolidation of Widgetworld and Widgetwonders.*

constraints (kun-STRAINTS): Specific restrictions that limit the quest to obtain an objective.

This factory has a number of constraints including an uneducated work force and machines that regularly break down.

consultant (kun-SULT-ent): An outsider with expertise in some area who spends time studying an organization and then offers advice for a price.

We have had three losing quarters in a row, so the board has hired a consultant to study the company.

consumer (kun-SUME-er): The one who uses a product. The consumer may also be the one who purchased the product. But sometimes, a purchase is made and then given to a consumer.

The consumer of Alpo in my house is my dog, Duke.

consumer confidence (kun-SUME-er KON-fih-dens): A survey of the way people feel about certain aspects of the economy—economic conditions, their future employment, and their personal finances. It is an attempt at measuring willingness to spend.

Before Christmas, many retailers were worried because the latest consumer confidence numbers showed people are still worried about the future.

Consumer Price Index (CPI) (kun-SUME-er price IN-dex): The same as cost of living index. A monthly government report on the prices of food, shelter, transportation, utilities, and other essentials. It is a way of studying inflation and is used to adjust Social Security payments. Many pension funds and cost-of-living increases depend on the CPI.

The CPI for the last three months has risen significantly. Some people are worried about all this inflation, but at least my pension checks are also going up.

consumption function (kun-SUMP-shun FUNK-shun): The mathematical ratio of consumption and earnings. Study has shown the two to be closely connected.

If you look at the consumption function for last year, you will see that consumer spending rose in those areas of the country where the economy was doing good.

contingency plan (kun-TIN-jen-se plan): A plan of action in case the unexpected happens.

We have a contingency plan in case the new line of widgets doesn't sell. The plan is to be ready to produce the old kind quickly.

contingent workers (kun-TIN-jent WERK-ers): People who work at a company to perform a specific one-time task and who are paid by the project.

When Frank started taking jobs from the temporary firm, he knew that being a contingent worker meant more freedom, and no benefits.

continuous production (kun-TIN-u-us pro-DUK-shun): A process in which raw materials continually go into production and come out as a standardized product.

The standard widget was produced by continuous production in which sheets of plastic and metal went in, and out came widgets.

contract (KON-tract): A binding agreement between two or more parties in which each promises goods or services in exchange for goods or services.

Sherry has a contract to design a brochure for Widgets Inc. Sherry has to design a suitable brochure before August 1, and Widgets Inc. must pay her $4,000.

contract date (KON-tract date): The date a contract is issued.

The contract date for that design project is June 30.

contractor (KON-tract-er): One who works by contract for whoever hires him rather than by paycheck for one specific company.

A physician is a contractor. So is someone who builds houses for individuals.

contributory (kun-TRIB-u-to-re): An employee benefit plan in which both employees and employers pay into, based on an agreed-upon percentage by both.

One of the reasons why Stanley likes working at a big company like Widgets Inc. is the contributory plan in which the company doubles everything he puts into the plan.

controllable costs (kun-TROLE-la-bl kosts): The costs that a department has some influence over are controllable costs. Other costs, such as the cost of an essential material, are not.

The boss ordered a closer watch on some controllable costs, especially overtime and travel allowance.

conversion ratio (kun-VER-zhun RA-she-o): When a convertible bond or preferred share is exchanged for common stock, the conversion ratio determines the amount of the trade.

I decided to trade my preferred stock for common stock now because the conversion ratio was good.

convertible mortgage (kun-VERT-ih-bl MOR-gej): A mortgage that can be changed to another type of mortgage within the term of the loan.

Sue and Bobby Snuggles started with an adjustable-rate mortgage but since it was also a convertible mortgage, they waited until the rates dropped and then locked in a fixed rate.

conveyance (kun-VAY-ans): Transfer of a title in real estate. All conveyances are recorded in the registry of deeds.

If you look up the last conveyance on that property, you will see that the title was transferred in 1991.

cooperative apartment (CO-OP): A real estate arrangement in which a buyer leases an apartment at a low rate and buys stock in the corporation that owns the building.

Sally was happy when her building went co-op because it meant she would now be investing instead of just paying a landlord.

copyright (KOP-e-rite): A protection that gives creative people such as artists and authors exclusive right to sell their work.

Patrick was worried that someone would steal his manuscript of his novel, so he got it copyrighted.

core business (kor BIZ-ness): The specialty of a company; the way it makes most of its money.

Widgets Inc. had diversified into so many areas, the consultant said he found it hard to figure out the core business anymore.

corner office (KOR-ner OFF-fiss): The place where the CEO works. Sometimes, the corner office is referred to as a living entity, meaning the CEO.

After the latest bad numbers were released in the quarterly report, many wondered what would be the next move to come out of the corner office.

corporate structure (KOR-po-rate STRUK-chure): The way a company is organized. The corporate structure includes all departments and the way authority is delegated throughout the company.

"The corporate structure of Widgets Inc. is so complex it is best to assume that two different departments in the company are not sharing information," said the consultant. "I recommend you contact each separately."

corporate veil (KOR-po-rate vale): Those who want to disguise their activity can use a corporate veil so that their identity is hidden.

It was difficult for authorities to catch Sam Slippery because he was adept at hiding his illegal actions behind a corporate veil.

corporate welfare (KOR-po-rate WEL-fair): Tax breaks that some corporations receive to do business in a certain country or state. Critics call those tax breaks corporate welfare.

The populist politician railed against corporate welfare and drew many cheers from the blue-collar crowd.

corporation (kor-po-RA-shun): A legal entity that exists separately from the owners. A corporation can sue or be sued, own property, or acquire debts. A corporation is legally like a person.

Decades ago when Jonathan Widget realized what he had invented, he formed a corporation to attract investors.

correction (kur-REK-shun): A reversal of a stock trend. If a stock price has been consistently rising above expectations and then falls back to where it was expected, it is said to have undergone a correction.

Yesterday's dramatic drop in the price of stock for Widgets Inc. was not all that unexpected. Experts called it a market correction for the past six months of rising prices.

cosign (co-SINE): Affixing a signature to a loan for another person. A person who cosigns a loan is responsible for payments if the person who took out the loan is unable to pay it.

When Todd graduated from college, he bought his first new car but he needed his father to cosign for the loan.

cost/benefit analysis (kost BEN-eh-fit ah-NAL-ih-sis): A comparison between the costs of doing something and the benefits of doing it. If the benefits outweigh the costs, it is worth doing.

If you do a cost/benefit analysis on that advertising campaign, you will see that it brought in ten times more money than it cost to produce.

cost containment (kost kun-TANE-ment): Using a specific stringent budget, and sticking with it.

> *"They're on a cost containment binge around here," complained Williams. "You can't even order pencils without it passing through three separate budgets."*

Cost of Living Index (Kost of LIV-ing IN-dex): The same as Consumer Price Index, CPI. A monthly government report on the prices of food, shelter, transportation, utilities, and other essentials. It is a way of studying inflation and is used to adjust Social Security payments. Many pension funds and cost-of-living increases depend on the Cost of Living Index.

> *The cost of living index shows that prices are rising quicker this year for essential items than they did last year.*

Cost of Living Adjustment (COLA) (kost of LIV-ing ad-JUST-ment): An adjustment of wages upward by a set formula based on inflationary changes in the Consumer Price Index. Some union contracts have these built in.

> *The way inflation is some years, you need to have a COLA.*

cost-recovery method (kost re-KUV-er-e METH-ud): A way of recognizing revenue in which all costs are paid for before any profit is recognized. Profit is not recognized as a percentage of each item sold. Instead, when payments come in they are applied to the cost of all items shipped. Once those are paid for, future payments are all gross profit.

> *We have a problem with collections, so we are doing our accounting with the cost-recovery method.*

counterclaim (COUNT-er-clame): A legal action by a defendant against a plaintiff. It is more than just an answer of a plaintiff's complaint. It is an actual charge by the defendant against the plaintiff.

> *When the two families sued the chemical plant, they didn't realize they would have to defend themselves against a counterclaim.*

countercyclical policy (COUNT-er-SIK-lik-ul POL-ih-se): Deliberate government actions to counteract the business cycle and, thus, keep growth steady.

Raising interest rates during inflation is countercyclical policy. The hope is that higher interest rates will drive down demand, which will drive down inflation.

counteroffer (COUNT-er-OFF-er): In negotiations, this is a response to an offer with a rejection and new offer.

When they heard what I wanted for a salary, they responded with a lower counteroffer.

covenant (KUV-eh-nent): An agreement, a promise, a contract, often with specific do's and don'ts.

We have a covenant stipulating that we will be paid twenty days after we complete the project.

cover the short position (KUV-er the short po-ZISH-un): Borrowing stocks, selling them, and then buying them back at a lower price and returning them to the owner.

When Jane bought 500 shares of Widgets Inc. after the price fell, she was covering the short position.

crash (krash): When the stock market falls a huge amount.

The market has been rising steadily for two years but many are afraid of a crash.

credit analyst (KRED-it AN-ah-list): A person who studies the finances of another person or a corporation to decide whether the applicant is a good risk for a loan.

The credit analyst saw that Shane Shiftless was late paying many bills and marked down that Shane would not be a good credit risk.

credit bureau (KRED-it BU-ro): A private company that keeps track of credit records of individuals and then sells that information for a fee.

Frank could not get a loan for a new car because the report from the credit bureau was not good.

credit rating (KRED-it RATE-ing): A formal appraisal of an individual's or a company's credit history and an evaluation of that person's or company's ability to repay future loans.

I have been good at paying bills on time for the past two years, so my credit rating has improved.

cross merchandising (kross MER-chun-dize-ing): A retailing ploy of setting up displays of two related products near each other. The idea is to lure customers from one product to a related product from the same company.

The tortilla chips from Mexican Specialties Company were set next to the salsa from the same company. It was a classic case of cross merchandising.

cubicle (KYU-bih-kl): A pretend private office set apart from others by a partition that is usually about five feet tall.

After another twelve-hour day, Sue complained, "Sometimes I feel like I live in this cubicle."

culture (KUL-chure): The prevailing habits and practices and attitude of an organization.

We have a loose culture here with a casual dress code and even after-work softball games. My last company had a stiff, formal culture.

current assumptions (KUR-rent as-SUMP-shuns): The use of current interest rates and mortality rates in devising life insurance premiums and benefits. This is considered more fair than using historical rates.

Based on current assumptions, your life insurance premiums will be higher this year than last.

current dollars (KUR-rent DOL-lurs): The price of an asset based on what it would cost new in the current market. The numbers are based on the consumer price index.

That car cost $10,000 ten years ago, but it would cost $20,000 in current dollars.

current ratio (KUR-rent RA-she-o): Current assets divided by current liabilities. If the ratio is high, there is more confidence in your ability to pay current debts.

Widgets Inc. has a high current ratio since its obligations are low and it has many assets.

cursor (KUR-sur): The blinking signal on a computer screen that shows where the next character will appear in the text.

If you want to add a sentence to that paragraph, you have to move the cursor to where you want to add it.

cusip number (KU-sip NUM-ber): The identification number on a stock certificate.

Besides his certificates, John was so meticulous that he kept two sets of records of the cusip numbers.

cutting edge (CUT-ing ej): At the forefront of new ideas, new technology, or new ways of operating.

We consider ourselves a cutting-edge company in the area of widget technology. If something is new, the chances are that we will be the ones introducing it.

cyberspace (SI-ber-spase): A destination without a location. Cyberspace is the world you travel to and through via your computer.

I have friends in cyberspace whom I have never talked with outside of my computer.

cyclical stocks (SIK-lik-ul stoks): Stocks that are most affected by the strength of the economy.

Automobile stocks are cyclical stocks because when the economy goes down, my consumers fear spending a lot for a new vehicle.

damages (DA-mij-es): The amount a plaintiff receives from a defendant in a tort-type court decision, or in a settlement.

Renee received $100,000 in damages from her former employer because her arm was amputated while working on a faulty machine.

data (DA-ta): Information that is collected.

We have some demographic data on the sales of widgets to teenagers that is very interesting.

database (DA-tah-base): The place on a computer that holds a collection of data that is available to many people for many uses.

We have records on every one of our customers, narrowed down to the income of the consumer matched with the price of the widget. As you can imagine, this is a database that many in our company want to access.

data interchange format (DIF) file (DA-tah in-ter-CHANGE FORmat): A way of transferring computer files from one system to another. This is often used for transferring spreadsheets or other accounting programs.

The accountant said to the CEO, "That's a DIF file so it's already set for you to get if you want it."

data processing (DA-tah PROSS-ess-ing): Transforming data into information by hand, by machine, or by computer.

We have an updated version of data processing on all of our computers. It's faster than the old version.

data transmission (DA-tah trans-MISH-un): The act of data being sent from one location to another.

> *In the old days the mail was our means of data transmission. Now, we use computers.*

dead-end job (ded end job): A job that is as good as it's going to get. There is no room for promotion or pay increases.

> *"I know this seems like a dead-end job," said one store clerk to another. "And for you it is a dead-end job. But not for me," he said, smiling. "My father owns this store."*

dead time (ded time): When a machine breaks or some other stoppage in operations occurs that causes a worker to be idle.

> *The electricity went out so there was a lot of dead time on the assembly line today.*

death (deth): For insurances, death requires a death certificate in order to pay death benefits.

> *When the millionaire was kidnapped and never found, it took years to declare death.*

debit (DEB-it): A debt, often entered on the left-hand side of an accounting ledger.

> *Add up all your debits and you will see what you owe.*

debug (de-BUG): Finding errors in computer programs and correcting them.

> *Smartypants Software wanted to announce they would be introducing five new games in a month, but first the engineers had to try to debug the games. "It may take a while," said one engineer.*

debt financing (det fi-NANS-ing): Raising money by borrowing money, such as with the sale of bonds.

We're going to build our new facility with some debt financing. We can handle a loan right now.

debt retirement (det re-TIRE-ment): Paying off a debt.

We need debt retirement on some of these old expenses before we can think about any new purchases.

debt service (det SERV-is): Amount of money needed to pay interest and any principal due for a year's time on a loan.

Little Widgets Company has a high annual debt service because the company needed a number of big loans to jump into the widget market.

deceptive practice (de-SEPT-iv PRAK-tis): Hiding facts, or even lying about facts.

When the insurance agent sold the Smiths a policy, he told them that it would cover anything that could possibly happen to them. They didn't find out until later that he was guilty of deceptive practice and that their policy didn't cover hardly anything.

deductible (de-DUKT-ih-bl): The amount of money an insured person or company must pay on an insurance claim. If a claim is for $10,000, and the deductible is $500, the insured receives a settlement of $9,500.

For my auto insurance, I have a $500 deductible.

deep pockets (deep POCK-ets): A lot of money to spend. If a company has deep pockets, it can survive a long period of poor performance.

Widgets Inc. will survive the recession. That company has deep pockets.

de facto (de-FAK-to): Something that exists in fact, but not by legal authority.

> *Before the authorities closed in, the three immigrants were running a de facto hospital in their neighborhood.*

default judgment (de-FAULT JUJ-ment): A court decision made against a defendant because the defendant failed to appear in court, or because the defendant did not answer a complaint.

> *The elderly plaintiffs won a default judgment against the telemarketing firm that sold them swamp land in Florida because the owners of the firm have skipped town.*

default setting (de-FAULT SET-ing): When there are a number of options on a computer and you choose none, the computer will automatically pick the default setting.

> *There are so many different page layouts to choose from in my word processing software, but I always use the default setting of a blank sheet with standard paragraphs.*

defeasance (de-FE-suns): To void a will or contract with a specific stipulation that was not met.

> *We were under contract to deliver 1,000 widgets a month for five years, but we are no longer obligated for the deliveries because of a defeasance that stated we must be paid for each delivery within thirty days. We have not been paid in months, so the contract is void.*

defective (de-FEK-tiv): Faulty.

> *Our biggest customer is outraged that we keep sending him defective widgets.*

Defense Research Institute (de-FENS re-SEARCH-IN-stih-tute): An organization of trial lawyers who specialize in defending against tort claims.

> *When Bigpolluter Inc. was sued by every environmental group in America, it turned to the Defense Research Institute for legal help.*

deferred credit (de-FERRED KRED-it): Income that has been received but not yet earned. An example would be an advance given for a project that has not yet started.

> *When I sold my first book, the advance was deferred credit. Once I had the money, I had to get to work. I also started having expenses on the project.*

deficit (DEF-ih-sit): A term for the difference that occurs when the U.S. government spends more than it takes in.

> *Every politician wants to eliminate the deficit, but none seem to know how to do it.*

deflation (de-FLA-shun): The opposite of inflation. When prices go down.

> *After a new technology has been around a few years, there is often deflation in the market.*

delinquency rate (de-LIN-kwen-se rate): A statistic showing the percentage of late payments out of the total number of loans in a portfolio.

> *The bank president called in Roger the loan officer because the loans he had approved had an unusually high delinquency rate.*

delivery (de-LIV-er-e): The physical transfer of a title.

> *The young husband said to his wife, "As soon as there is delivery, we will own a new house."*

Delphi Technique (DEL-fi tek-NEKE): A way to hold a meeting without holding a meeting. With a coordinator in charge, all members of a group submit ideas about a problem to the coordinator. The coordinator arranges all the comments into a report and submits them back to the group members. The group members then comment on all the comments and submit them back to the coordinator, who tries to use the comments to reach a consensus.

We need to figure out how to speed up our widget assembly line but we don't have time for a meeting. We will use the Delphi Technique instead, so submit your comments by Wednesday to Ann Smith, who will be the coordinator.

demographics (deh-mo-GRAF-iks): A statistical study of population that breaks down into age, income, location, or other factors.

When Widgets Inc. studied the demographics of their customers, they found that more than half of their customers were middle-aged males in the South who like country music.

demoralize (de-MOR-ul-ize): To bring down the morale of a group.

The boss's raving about little errors had a tendency to demoralize everybody.

departmentalization (de-part-MEN-tul-ize-a-shun): The method of splitting employees into groups that are each responsible for different tasks.

As Widgets Inc. has grown, the company has so much departmentalization that if you want to order pencils you have to submit forms to five different departments.

deregulation (de-REG-u-la-shun): Removing government regulations from an industry for the purpose of letting the market determine prices.

After deregulation in the airline industry, prices went down as airliners tried to capture a bigger share of the market.

derivatives (de-RIV-ah-tivs): An investment that doesn't follow a specific commodity but is based upon a complex mathematical equation related to a market.

Many investors do not understand derivatives but they put their money in them in the hope that the market will react a certain way.

detail person (de-TAIL PER-sun): A salesperson who works with existing customers to make sure the customer is happy with the details of the product and sale.

Every few weeks, Widgets Inc. was called on by a detail person who discussed the operation of the new machinery and worked to make sure it was operating as the company ordered.

diminishing returns (dih-MIN-ish-ing re-TERNS): A law of production which states that at some point increased staff and machinery will not be equaled by an equal increase in productivity. The reason for the law is inexperience and waste expected with a larger facility and work force.

The board of Widgets Inc. decided it was not worth expanding the factory for the fourth time in five years because of the law of diminishing returns.

direct cost (dih-REKT cost): Physical costs for a product.

The direct costs of widget making include materials and wages. The indirect costs include interest and insurance.

direct mail (dih-REKT mail): A form of advertising in which customers are sent mail about a product, often in a form that appears to be a personal letter.

Widgets Inc. is launching a direct-mail campaign aimed at middle-aged men in the South who like country music because those customers have historically been most responsive to a pitch from the company.

discharge (dis-CHARJ): To fulfill the obligations of a contract or debt.

When Sue turned in the project, she was discharged from the contract.

disclosure (dis-KLO-zhur): Revealing all information that has a bearing on a company's financial status.

The disclosure of three lost contracts in the last quarter weighed heavily on some investor's minds.

discontinuance of plan (dis-kun-TIN-u-uns of plan): The termination of a pension plan, only allowed as a matter of business necessity.

When Widgets Inc. filed for bankruptcy, employees found out about the discontinuance of their pension plan.

discontinued operation (dis-kun-TIN-ude op-er-A-shun): The end of a business segment. In accounting, the numbers from a discontinued operation are figured separately from continuing operations.

The widgets that were marketed to young Asian females didn't sell, so that line is a discontinued operation.

discount (dis-COUNT): A way of issuing securities so that they are sold at less than face value and redeemed at the end of a certain period of time at face value.

The bond is discounted now, but in five years you can redeem it at face value.

discovery period (dis-KUV-er-e PEH-re-ud): The amount of time after a policy ends in which a principal that was formerly insured is allowed to report a loss that occurred while the policy was effective.

The discovery period for the old policy covering the widget factory is one year.

discretionary cost (dis-KREH-shun-ah-re cost): Costs that vary depending on management decisions. These costs include advertising, and research and development.

Times are tough at Widgets Inc. so management has ordered cuts in all discretionary costs.

discretionary income (dis-KREH-shun-ah-re IN-kum): Money a person has to spend from their income after they have paid for necessities such as food, shelter, and clothing.

Three years after college, John was finally making enough money to have some discretionary income. He decided to take a trip with some of the extra money.

discretionary policy (dis-KREH-shun-ah-re POL-ih-se): Government economic policy that is not governed by a set of regulations but is set by humans.

Adding to the money supply is one example of discretionary policy by the Federal Reserve Board.

discrimination (dis-krim-ih-NA-shun): The unfair treatment of individuals because of their race, religion, sex, sexual orientation, or ethnic background.

Widgets Inc. has 2,000 employees and all of them are white males. Many women and minorities who have applied for jobs with Widgets Inc. say the company is guilty of discrimination.

disinflation (dis-in-FLA-shun): A slowing of the rate of inflation. When the rate that prices increase slows down, it is disinflation. It is different from "deflation," which is a drop in prices.

Inflation is slowing down. Some analysts say the disinflation is due to low demand for high-priced items.

dismemberment benefit (dis-MEM-ber-ment BEN-eh-fit): The amount of cash that a person collects from health insurance for losing a body part. Different body parts are worth different amounts of money.

Jack Armless was paid a dismemberment benefit after his terrible accident in the Widget factory.

disposable income (dis-POS-ah-bl in-KUM): Personal income remaining after taxes have been paid.

Most of my disposable income goes toward paying for rent, food, utilities, and gas for my car.

distress price (dis-TRESS prise): When a firm is in trouble and is offered a price for an item that it would not normally accept, but which it must accept in order to have some income to continue operations, the price is a distress price.

The manager shrugged. "We will distress price those widgets if it will bring in enough money to keep the plant running."

distribution (dis-trih-BU-shun): The way goods are moved from a manufacturer.

There is an overload of widgets in California but nobody can find them anywhere in Texas. Something is wrong with our distribution.

distributor (dis-TRIB-u-tur): A person or company who acts as a middleman between a manufacturer and a retailer. A distributor usually has a warehouse full of items from many manufacturers.

The owner of the store told his assistant manager to call the distributor and order more widgets.

diversify (di-VER-sih-fi): In investments, to diversify is to spread your money out into many categories in order to reduce risk. In business, to diversify is to be involved in many different businesses.

> *Juanita had all of her money in Widgets Inc. stock but her financial advisor had recommended to diversify in case the company had problems. Or . . . Widgets Inc. released a new line of widgets, as well as baked goods and children's toys. Some analysts say the company has diversified too much and has lost focus.*

dividend (DIV-ih-dend): The amount of profits that shareholders receive from a corporation.

> *When I get my dividend check from Widgets Inc., we can go on a vacation to Europe. The company had a tremendous quarter.*

dividend payout (DIV-ih-dend PAY-out): The percentage of a company's earnings that are paid out in dividends.

> *Widgets Inc. is a big, stable company that has a high dividend payout.*

doing business as (DBA) (DO-ing BIZ-ness az): An assumed name one uses for a business.

> *You can transfer the title of that car to John Smith DBA Smith Taxi.*

dollar drain (DOL-lur drane): When a country imports more from the United States than it exports, its dollars drain away.

> *We make the best widgets in the world, so widget manufacturing is an industry causing a dollar drain across the globe.*

DOS (dos): Disk Operating System. A program that runs a computer.

> *We design software to run on DOS.*

dot matrix printer (dot MA-trix PRINT-er): A printer that forms characters from a series of connected dots.

> *I have a good dot matrix printer but it does not have the quality of the newer laser printers.*

double click (DUH-bl klik): How to call up a file on a Windows screen with a computer mouse. To click the left mouse button twice in a row is to double click.

> *The computer instructor said, "Just double click on what you want to call up and the file will show up on your screen."*

double dipping (DUH-bl DIP-ing): Retired military personnel who receive a military pension but also work a civilian job are double dipping.

> *When Mona retired from the Navy, and began receiving her pension, she was happy to take a computer job and start double dipping.*

double-entry bookkeeping (DUH-bl EN-tre BOOK-keep-ing): Accounting method that requires entering an item in at least two accounts.

> *Make sure you record the cost of widget parts under general supplies and under widget parts. We are doing double-entry bookkeeping.*

Dow Jones (dow jones): A financial information services company. The publisher of the *Wall Street Journal*, and the issuer of financial data.

> *Sue was proud of her son who graduated from Harvard and then landed a job with Dow Jones.*

Dow Jones Industrial Average (dow jones in-DUS-tre-ul AV-er-uj): A market indicator that studies the stock of thirty major industrial companies. It is referred to sometimes as "the Dow," and it is closely watched.

> *The Dow Jones Industrial Average fell by thirty points today. Some analysts fear it may portend the beginning of a recession.*

down (down): A computer that is not working is down.

I hope this computer will not be down for long because I have a lot of work to do.

download (DOWN-lode): Transmitting a computer file from a network computer to a personal computer.

Linda gets mad whenever her husband downloads pictures of pretty girls.

downscale (DOWN-skale): Changing the focus of a business to lower-income customers.

After fifty years in Beverly Hills, Snooty Clothes is going downscale to try to capture more customers.

downsizing (DOWN-size-ing): Shrinking a company by laying people off.

The folks at Widgets Inc. were hearing rumors that their company would soon undergo a downsizing, so everyone was scrambling to put together their resumes.

dry goods (dri goods): Clothing, fabrics, and textiles.

The market for dry goods is always pretty strong.

dumping (DUMP-ing): The process of selling goods in a foreign market below price for the purpose of capturing a share of that market from foreign competition, or to sell inferior goods that could not be sold in the U.S.

Widgets Inc. has been dumping their inferior widgets in underdeveloped parts of Asia.

duplication of benefits (du-plih-KA-shun of BEN-eh-fits): When two different health insurance policies cover the same loss. The policies share the cost, or one policy becomes the primary policy while the other becomes the secondary policy.

> *My injury at work was covered by the company's policy as well as the policy I have through my wife's place of employment. I don't know what will happen about this duplication of benefits.*

duress (du-RESS): Action that makes someone do what they otherwise would not do.

> *Bob signed the confession under duress since he was being blackmailed because he was having an affair.*

duty (DU-te): A tax on the importing or exporting of goods.

> *You have to pay a duty on the widgets you import from Japan.*

eager beaver (E-ger BE-ver): An enthusiastic employee who will do any extra work and is anxious for advancement.

> *Ralph works every holiday and every weekend. He sure is an eager beaver.*

early retirement (ER-le re-TIRE-ment): To stop working before normal retirement age. There is usually a reduction in the monthly retirement benefit.

> *When Robert's grandchildren moved to his hometown, he decided he wanted to take an early retirement to spend time with them.*

early trading (ER-le TRADE-ing): Trading early in the day, before noon.

> *Stock prices went up in early trading.*

early withdrawal penalty (ER-le with-DRAW-ul PEN-ul-te): The amount an investor must pay to remove money from a fixed-term investment before it matures.

Sheila knew there would be an early withdrawal penalty for taking money from her ten-year certificate of deposit, but she had to do it anyway because she needed the money to bail out her brother.

earned income (erned IN-kum): Income that is derived from work, rather than income that comes from dividends.

Sally Spooninmouth has zero earned income but she inherited 100,000 shares of Widgets Inc., so she doesn't need a job.

earnings and profits (ERN-ings and PROF-its): The ability of a corporation to make dividend payments to shareholders.

Widgets Inc. has consistently high earnings and profits, which is why I invested in the company.

earnings per share (EPS): (ern-ings per share): The amount of a company's profits that are given to each share of common stock.

I'm glad I bought extra shares of Widgets Inc. last year because the company had such a good year and the earnings per share has gone way up.

earnings report (ern-ings re-PORT): A report that a publicly held company issues about its earnings.

Before you buy any stock in Widgets Inc., you should read the latest earnings report.

earthquake insurance (erth KWAKE in-SHURE-ens): An add-on to a standard insurance policy to cover against damage from earthquakes.

In California, the Widgets Inc. factory pays a high premium for earthquake insurance.

easy money (EZE-e MUN-e): A government economic policy that increases the national money supply to lower interest rates and make loans easier to get.

The easy money policies of the past few years have contributed to the growth of inflation.

economic efficiency (e-ko-NOM-ik e-FISH-en-se): The ability of a company to put its resources to the best use and to distribute goods at the lowest possible cost.

The goal of this company is to operate at full economic efficiency.

economic growth rate (e-ko-NOM-ik grothe rate): The annual percentage rate of change in the Gross Domestic Product, or GDP.

The economic growth rate will be an issue in this year's presidential election.

economic loss (e-ko-NOM-ik loss): When a company cannot produce enough profits to stay in business.

This company is suffering too much of an economic loss. We have to close.

economic sanctions (e-ko-NOM-ik SANK-chuns): When one country opposes some policy of another country, the first country can try to punish the second by imposing tariffs or even refusing to buy goods from or sell goods to that country. Such leverage is an economic sanction.

The U.S. first tried to use economic sanctions against Iraq to get its troops to leave Kuwait.

economies of scale (e-KON-uh-mees of skale): The ability of a company to produce a huge amount of an item, thereby making the cost lower per item. Thus, a big company can often produce an item cheaper than smaller competitors.

We can produce the least expensive widgets in the world because of our economies of scale.

edict (E-dikt): An official proclamation or policy statement from a company.

The president issued an edict that no widgets will leave the factory before being inspected twice.

effective date (ef-FEKT-iv date): The date of an agreement.

I only have a few more days off and then I have to start my new job. It is late October and the effective date of my contract is November 1.

efficiency (e-FISH-en-se): An assessment of the productivity of a human worker or of a machine in relation to the effort put in.

We called in a consultant to do an efficiency study of all aspects of our factory.

efficient market (ef-FIH-shint MARK-et): A theory that suggests it is impossible to beat the market because the market has been thoroughly analyzed and all investors have access to the same information.

The widget market is an efficient market that has been studied for years. It will go up, but no one will be surprised.

egress (E-gress): An exit from a building, or to exit a building.

The planning commission was concerned that there are not enough proposed means of egress for the new restaurant.

elasticity of demand (e-las-TIS-ih-te of de-MAND): The way buyers respond to a change in price. It is a ratio of the change in percentage of the number of units purchased versus the change in percentage of price.

Widgets are an essential item, so people will buy them no matter how much the price goes up. There is not much elasticity of demand.

elasticity of supply (e-las-TIS-ih-te of sup-PLI): The way output responds to a change in price. It is the ratio of the percentage change in the number of items supplied versus the percentage change in price.

If we lower prices we are prepared to increase productivity quite a bit. We have large elasticity of supply.

electronic bulletin board (e-lekt-TRON-ik BUL-leh-tin bord): A posting, often within a company, of information in a computer database that is of interest and is accessible to all.

The latest job listings are posted on the Widgets Inc. electronic bulletin board.

electronic mail (e-mail) (e-lekt-TRON-ik mail): A system that allows people at computers to write each other messages that can be sent instantaneously from one computer to another.

As soon as I finish putting together the agenda for next week's meeting, I will e-mail it to you.

electronic publishing (e-lekt-TRON-ik PUB-lish-ing): To put a document into a format that can be read on a computer screen. It could be in CD-ROM format, on a computer disk, or on the World Wide Web.

We wanted to get information out about Widgets Inc. to as many people as possible so we have published a full-color brochure on the wonders of widgets and we are looking into ways of electronic publishing as well.

eligibility period (EL-ih-jih-BIL-ih-te PEH-re-ud): The amount of time a new employee is given to apply for health or life insurance and pay a first premium without being required to first take a physical examination. After that time, the employee may be required to have a physical examination and then may be required to pay a higher premium.

The eligibility period for insurance with Widget Inc.'s carrier is thirty days.

eligibility requirements (EL-ih-jih-BIL-ih-te re-KWIRE-ments): Conditions in employee benefit plans that must be met before those plans kick in for that employee.

> *The eligibility requirement for our pension plan is that you must have worked full time for Widgets Inc. for at least fifteen years.*

embezzlement (em-BEZ-zl-ment): The stealing of property from an employer for personal use.

> *Sue took a dollar a day home from the bank she worked at as a teller for twenty straight years before she was caught and charged with embezzlement.*

emerging markets (e-MERJ-ing MARK-ets): Markets in underdeveloped countries that are expanding rapidly, or markets in new technologies that are expanding.

> *Widgets Inc. is opening a factory in Africa because it is an emerging market.*

eminent domain (EM-ih-nent do-MANE): The taking of private property for public use.

> *When the state wanted to build a new highway, it took hundreds of homes by eminent domain.*

Employee Assistance Program (EAP) (em-PLOY-e as-SIST-uns PRO-gram): Programs offered by companies to help employees deal with personal problems such as substance abuse.

> *After Eddie was arrested for drunk driving for the second time, he entered an employee assistance program which helped him overcome his problem.*

Employee Retirement Income Security Act of 1974 (ERISA) (em-PLOY-e re-TIRE-ment IN-kum seh-KYU-rih-te akt): A law controlling the operation of private pension plans to make sure the plans are fair and safe.

> *The pension plan at Widgets Inc. is in good shape partly because it is managed well and partly because it must be managed well because of ERISA regulations.*

Employee Stock Ownership Plan (ESOP) Trust (em-PLOY-e stok OWN-ership plan): Program that allows and encourages employees to purchase stock in the company.

> *I was glad to get a job at Widgets Inc. because they have an ESOP plan.*

empowered employees (em-POW-erd em-PLOY-ees): Employees who are given decision-making responsibilities in a company.

> *Widgets Inc. knows that empowered employees will work harder and care more about the company. That's why management is always asking employees how to make operations run smoother.*

encoding (en-KODE-ing): Hiding a message from general readership by putting it into a certain code.

> *I'll be sending along a report of recommendations of which employees should be laid off, and I'll be encoding the message because of its sensitive nature.*

encumbrance (en-KUM-brens): Any restriction on the use of a property that diminishes its worth.

> *That is a nice piece of land except for the easement that allows a state highway to be built through the middle of it any time in the next 100 years. That easement is an encumbrance that you should consider before purchasing it.*

endowment (en-DOW-ment): A gift of money or property that is to be used for a specific purpose as set forth by the giver.

Jonathan Widget left an endowment of $1 million to his hometown toward construction of the Widget Library.

engineering (en-jeh-NEER-ing): The planning, designing, construction, and management of a physical project.

Take the idea for a new building to the folks in engineering to get their input.

enterprise (EN-ter-prize): A business project, or a business firm.

The Johnson brothers went into advertising and they've been pretty good at that enterprise. Or . . . There is a new enterprise, Johnson Advertising Company, that seems to have good people running it.

enterprise zone (EN-ter-prize zone): A geographic area outlined by the government. Businesses are offered special tax incentives to relocate into the zone, which is often in a neglected urban area that needs jobs.

The new Widgets Inc. factory was located in an enterprise zone because it meant low taxes, good public relations, and a large pool of workers to choose from for the labor force.

entrepreneur (ahn-tr-preh-NUHR): A person who starts a business.

Jonathan Widget was an entrepreneur, but the company now is a conglomerate run by a huge bureaucracy.

enure (en-URE): An insurance clause that states that benefits go to the insured.

My car was broken into at the repair shop but I received the benefit, not the repair shop, because my policy had an enure clause.

Equal Employment Opportunity Commission (EEOC) (E-kwul em-PLOY-ment op-pur-TU-nih-te kum-MISH-un): The federal agency responsible for making sure there is no discrimination in hiring or firing workers.

> *Sue thought she was passed over for a promotion because she was a woman, so she filed a complaint with the EEOC.*

equal opportunity employer (E-kwul op-pur-TU-nih-te em-PLOY-er): An employer that has promised not to discriminate.

> *Widgets Inc. is an equal opportunity employer.*

equilibrium (e-kwih-LIB-re-um): A steady market in which no outside forces are affecting its direction.

> *"If everything except prices remains in equilibrium, prices will still change," said the professor. "Because prices always change."*

equity (EK-wih-te): The amount of value currently held in a property.

> *We gained a lot of equity in our house when the value rose from $100,000 to $250,000.*

equity method (EK-wih-te METH-ud): A method of accounting used by major investors in the common stock of a company. If someone has between 20 percent and 50 percent of the stock in a company, the equity method is used. This method shows investee profits in the accounting book, but the same number is a debit, investee dividends, for tax purposes.

> *Harriet Widget, great-granddaughter of Jonathan Widget, doesn't get to many board meetings. She is just happy that the company uses the equity method for her dividends.*

ergonomics (er-go-NOM-iks): The science of designing a workplace to increase the safety, comfort, and productivity of workers.

> *Looking around his office surroundings, Trent thought the place could use the help of someone who understands ergonomics.*

escalator clause (ES-kah-la-tur klauz): A clause in a contract that calls for changes in the contract if certain things happen. A union could put in one tied to the cost of living, or one could be put in a lease tied to utility costs.

Inflation doesn't worry me as much as it used to because my union has an escalator clause in our current contract.

escape key (es-CAPE): A key on a computer keyboard titled "Esc." In many programs, hitting this key will allow you to quit a program.

When you're done using Widget Wars, the hot new game by Smartypants Software, all you have to do to quit the program is hit "escape."

escrow account (ES-kro uh-COUNT): The place where a third party holds assets before they are transferred from one party to another.

Paul's inheritance was held in escrow until he turned twenty-five. It's a good thing, or he probably would have spent all of it when he was eighteen.

estate (es-TATE): Everything you own. When you die, you leave an estate.

If you are rich and die, you leave a large estate and increased odds that your loved ones will tussle over how it is divided.

estate planning (es-TATE PLAN-ing): The efficient art of planning for the financial aspect of your death. It includes drawing a will, and setting up different accounts such as trust funds. The idea is for your heirs to avoid paying as much in taxes as possible.

William thought estate planning was gruesome but his wife said it was the nicest thing they could do for their kids. "Who do you want to have the money? The kids or the government?"

estimated tax (ES-tih-mated tax): Quarterly payments of estimated income tax due. This must be for all income received that was not subject to withholding tax.

When Andy quit the design firm and started freelancing, he had to begin paying an estimated tax.

ethics (ETH-iks): Doing the right thing for the proper moral reason.

Zach must not have any ethics, since he took widgets home for his own use.

Eurobanking (U-ro-BANK-ing): Banking that involves dealing in many different currencies.

The new branch office of Moneyhungry Bank will be near the airport and involved in Eurobanking.

eviction (e-VIK-chun): The physical ouster of someone from a piece of property by weight of authority or legal proceedings.

We tried to get the Smith family to move out of the apartment, but they refused to leave. It's time to start an eviction.

exchange (ex-CHANJE): Securities are traded on an exchange.

Widgets Inc. stock is listed on the New York Stock Exchange.

exchange rate (ex-CHANJE rate): The price that one country's currency trades for another country's currency.

The exchange rate of the dollar against the wooden shebango of the island nation of Paradise is 1-1. A dollar trades equally with a wooden shebango.

excise tax (ex-SIZE tax): A tax that is not deductible. It is the tax on everything besides property and income. You pay an excise tax when you buy something.

My car is registered in the town of Widgetville and I have to pay an excise tax to the town.

exclusion (ex-KLU-zhun): Something that is not covered by an insurance policy.

"My homeowners' policy had an exclusion for tornadoes," said the distraught person on the news.

exclusive remedy (ex-KLU-siv REM-eh-de): A situation in which an employee is injured and the employer is liable for the injury, but the employee is not allowed to sue the employer.

Stan could not sue Widgets Inc. for injuries he suffered while working in the factory. The exclusive remedy he received was workers' compensation.

executive (ex-EK-u-tiv): A top manager responsible for many decisions.

When Anthony talked with the executives at Widgets Inc. he noticed that they were very confident and that they all wore expensive shoes. It's gotta be the shoes, he thought.

executive committee (ex-EK-u-tiv kum-MIT-te): A group of top executives that establishes policy, plans, and can request justification for certain actions.

There is an executive committee at Widgets Inc. studying ways to break into foreign markets.

executive perks (ex-EK-u-tiv perks): Special treatment given to executives.

Molly was enticed to work for Widgets Inc. because of the executive perks such as the use of the company yacht and company jet.

executor (EX-eh-ku-tur): The person in charge of divvying up an estate as directed by a will.

Since Samuel was the oldest child, he was the executor of his father's will.

exemption (ex-EMP-shun): A deduction given to a taxpayer because of a specific situation that is tax deductible. For instance, a child is a dependency exemption.

When Sue became pregnant in January, her husband, Harry the accountant, was happy the child would be born this year to give them another exemption.

exercise (EX-er-size): When you have an option in a contract and you use that right.

We leased the house with an option to buy anytime in the next five years. Well, interest rates have come down so I think we should exercise that right.

exhaustive (egz-AWS-tiv): Looking at all possible scenarios and outcomes.

We did an exhaustive search before we hired Cynthia to be our new president.

exit interview (EX-it IN-ter-vu): A final interview with an employee before that employee leaves the company. The interview covers the operation of the company and it is expected the employee would be brutally honest.

After Stephanie was laid off, she finally had the courage in her exit interview to tell how her supervisor verbally abused her.

ex officio (ex of-FISH-e-o): A title that is held by virtue of holding another office.

As president of the company, Brenda is an ex officio member of the board, therefore there is no reason to appoint her.

expense (ex-PENS): A business cost that is deductible. An expense comes from operations or maintenance, not capital expenditures.

Our expense for utilities is sky-high this year because we kept the factory open twenty-four hours a day.

expense account (ex-PENS uh-COUNT): Allowance given to employees to pay for travel and for business entertainment.

Ed took a new client out to dinner and billed it to his expense account.

expense budget (ex-PENS BUDJ-et): The amount allocated for expenses for a certain time period.

The company is cutting costs so the expense budget has been cut by 20 percent.

experience curve (ex-PEH-re-ens kurv): The phenomenon in which production costs per unit go down while the number of units produced increases. This assumes employees will be more productive and supplies will cost less at a higher volume.

Widgets Inc. is making a larger profit than its competitors because of its experience curve.

experience rating (ex-PEH-re-ens RATE-ing): A way of calculating the rate of insurance premiums for a specific group by studying the statistical loss experience of the group.

Auto insurance rates for sixteen-year-old males are high because of the experience rating of that demographic group.

expert power (EX-pert POW-er): The ability to influence a decision because of one's knowledge.

The consultant we hired agrees with me about changes that must be made on the production floor. Maybe the board will listen to him because he has expert power.

expert system (EX-pert SIS-tem): A computer program that is designed to simulate the thought process of an expert in a particular field.

Doctors often use expert systems when considering putting their patient through an operation.

expert witness (EX-pert WIT-ness): A person who is called to testify in court because he or she has an expertise about some particular area.

It seemed people were lining up to be expert witnesses in the O.J. Simpson trial.

exploitation (ex-ploy-TA-shun): Being unfair to an employee for one's own benefit.

Widgets Inc. was charged with exploitation for paying its female workers only half of what its comparable male employees earned.

exponential smoothing (ex-po-NEN-shul SMOOTH-ing): A method of short-term forecasting in which past data is used to predict the future. More weight is given to recent data than is given to data from the past, since it is assumed recent data will have more of a bearing on future performance.

If you do some exponential smoothing, you will see that the future is bright even though profits were off two years ago. This year has been good, and that bodes well for the future.

exposure (ex-PO-zhur): The amount of money at risk in an investment, Or . . . The amount of media play a particular item receives.

My exposure from my investment in common stock in Widgets Inc. is great but I believe in the company. Or . . . There has been a lot of exposure for our new widgets because the media is so fascinated by the development.

Express Mail (ex-PRESS mail): Next-day delivery guaranteed by the U.S. Postal Service.

Send the draft of the report to me by Express Mail because I need to review it tomorrow.

extended coverage (ex-TEND-ed KUV-er-ehj): Insurance coverage that covers items not covered in a standard policy.

When the tornado hit, we were glad our policy included extended coverage.

extension (ex-TEN-shun): An agreement to lengthen the time of a contract.

John was so successful in his first year that the board offered him an extension on his contract.

extenuating circumstances (ex-TEN-u-ate-ing SIR-kum-stan-ses): Uncommon situation causing a project not to be finished on time.

I would have had the report done on time but there were some extenuating circumstances. My dog ate the first draft.

external audit (ex-TER-nul AW-dit): An examination of a company's finances by an outside, independent firm or person.

The board decided it wanted an external audit to ensure the numbers it has received from management are correct.

external documents (ex-TER-nul DOK-u-ments): Documents, such as invoices, that have been handled by outsiders but are necessary for the record-keeping of a company.

The auditor wanted to see all external documents associated with the new construction project.

extractive industry (ex-TRAKT-iv IN-dus-tre): An industry that is involved in taking things out of the ground.

The coal industry is an extractive industry.

extraordinary item (ex-TROR-dih-nah-re I-tem): Something unusual that must be explained to shareholders.

One extraordinary item that was explained to investors was that one of Widget Inc.'s top executives had embezzled $100,000 last quarter.

extrapolation (ex-trap-o-LA-shun): A prediction of future numbers based on the trend of past numbers.

By extrapolation, you will see that last year's good numbers should mean great numbers this year.

fabricator (FAB-rih-ka-tur): One who creates a product out of raw material.

I am a fabricator at Widgets Inc. because I turn raw plastic into widgets.

facade (fah-SOD): The front outside wall of a building.

We're going to change the facade of our building to give it a more classy look.

face value (fase VAL-u): The amount written on a financial instrument. If a check is written out for $100, the face value is $100.

The face value of the savings bond is $50 when it matures in seven years. Right now, its market value is little more than the $25 I paid for it.

factory overhead (FAK-to-re O-ver-HED): Utilities, maintenance, insurance and other costs incurred for the running of a factory.

Widgets are not dangerous to make, therefore our insurance is low, which helps keep down our factory overhead.

failure analysis (FAIL-ure ah-NAL-ih-sis): A study of an unmet goal.

The output of our factory didn't even come close to the goals we set. It's time to do a failure analysis and figure out why.

Fair Labor Standards Act (FLSA) (fair LA-bur STAND-urds akt): The 1938 law that set the minimum wage per hour and the maximum hours worked before receiving overtime pay.

You have to pay at least minimum wage or you violate the Fair Labor Standards Act.

fair market value (fair MARK-et VAL-u): The price that something sells for when both buyer and seller are acting of their own free will.

I would say I received fair market value for the antique widgets because I sold them at an auction.

fair rate of return (fair rate of re-TERN): The profit that a regulated utility is allowed to earn.

The electric company is trying to get the utilities commission to raise the fair rate of return, but a group of citizens has banned together to fight the rate increase.

fair trade (fair trade): A price agreement between a manufacturer and a retailer stating an item will be sold at or above a specified price.

The widgets at Widgetworld must be sold for at least $7.99 apiece because of a fair trade agreement with Widgets Inc.

fallback option (FALL-bak OP-chun): A secondary plan in case the primary plan fails.

The company needs a fallback option in case the new advertising strategy doesn't work.

false advertising (fals AD-ver-tize-ing): Misleading descriptions of products or services.

When Widgets Inc. hyped their product as fun to play with and a cure for the common cold, it was false advertising.

family branding (FAM-ih-le BRAND-ing): Giving the same name to a number of products to encourage recognition and name-brand loyalty.

We're coming out with a new line of doohickeys but we're going to put the Widgets brand on it because family branding should help any new products we develop.

Family and Medical Leave Act (FMLA) (FAM-ih-le and MED-ik-ul leev akt): A federal law affecting employers with fifty or more employees. The law requires employers to allow employees to take leave for specific family and medical reasons.

When John's first child was born, he was allowed to be home with his wife and child for a few weeks because of the Family and Medical Leave Act.

family history (FAM-ih-le HIS-to-re): A study of family background of diseases for health and medical insurance. The idea is to see if the person is susceptible to hereditary disease.

Julie was afraid that her new insurance company would do a family history and discover all the cancer that has devastated her family, and then maybe raise her premiums.

family of funds (FAM-ih-le of funds): Different mutual funds managed by the same investment firm.

I am going to look into investing in one of the funds in the Fidelity family of funds.

fast tracking (fast TRAK-ing): Setting chosen employees on a schedule of fast promotions and increased responsibilities while most workers are bypassed.

Ever since the company started fast tracking my old friend Ellen, she walks around with a superior air.

faux pas (fo-PAH): A social mistake of either words or a deed.

At the company Christmas party, Bill committed a faux pas when he spilled beer on the wife of the CEO.

favorable trade balance (FA-ver-ah-bl trade BAL-ens): When you are exporting more in dollar value than you are importing.

The U.S. has a favorable trade balance with the Island of Paradise because all that the island exports is bananas, but they import the conveniences of modern life.

fax (fax): A machine that uses telephone lines to transmit printed material to another fax machine. The machine electronically scans the material to be sent, and sends electric signals by phone line to another machine, which reads those signals and reproduces the document.

Archie, in his office in San Francisco, asked Reggie, in his office in New York, to fax him the report.

feather one's nest (FETH-er wons nest): Illegally taking company funds and putting them in a private account for the future.

Theodore tried to feather his nest but he was caught. His new nest is a jail cell.

Federal Deposit Insurance Corporation (FDIC) (FED-er-ul de-POZ-it in-SHURE-ens kor-po-RA-shun): The Federal Agency established during the depression that insures depositors for up to $100,000. The account has to be in a member bank.

When I started hearing rumors my bank might close, I was not too worried because it has FDIC insurance. Luckily, it never closed, so it didn't matter. But it was good to know it's there.

federal farm credit system (FED-er-ul farm KRED-it SIS-tem): A federal system to provide credit to farmers.

There are twelve farm credit districts in the federal farm credit system.

federal funds (FED-er-ul funds): Money that commercial banks put in Federal Reserve Banks.

There are reserve requirements for banks to keep money in the Federal Reserve.

Federal Housing Administration (FHA) (FED-er-ul HOUSE-ing ad-min-is-TRA-shun): A federal agency that gives out loans to help people get into housing.

All that elderly housing on Oak Street is an FHA project.

Federal Insurance Contributions Act (FICA) (FED-er-ul in-SHURE-ens kon-trih-BU-shuns akt): The federal law that calls for paying Social Security tax.

Zeke is self-employed but he still has to make steep FICA payments.

Federal National Mortgage Administration (FNMA, also known as Fannie Mae) (FED-er-ul NAH-shun-ul MOR-gej ad-min-is-TRA-shun): A federal agency that purchases mortgages from lenders and resells them to buyers.

Our first house was a Fannie Mae house.

Federal Reserve System (FED-er-ul re-SERV SIS-tem): The federal bank, made up of twelve regional banks that regulate commercial banks in their regions. The Federal Reserve System regulates the money supply, examines bank records, and acts as a clearinghouse for transfers of money from bank to bank.

Investors are curious if the Federal Reserve System is going to alter the money supply.

federal tax lien (FED-er-ul tax leen): If you owe taxes to the federal government for your property but don't pay them, the government can place a federal tax lien against that property.

When the government placed a federal tax lien on his property, Joe figured it was time to move to Montana.

Federal Trade Commission (FTC) (FED-er-ul trade kum-MISH-un): A federal agency charged with ensuring free and fair competition and with preventing unfair or deceptive acts of commerce such as price-fixing agreements.

The FTC will be very interested in the proposed merger of Widgets Inc. and Stuff Company.

Federal Unemployment Tax Act (FED-er-ul un-em-PLOY-ment tax akt): The legislation that created federal unemployment insurance.

> *When Ethel was laid off from Smartypants Software, she was happy for the federal unemployment tax act.*

fee (fe): The price charged by a professional service.

> *My laywer's fee is quite high, but he's worth it.*

feeding frenzy (FEED-ing FREN-ze): When a stock's price starts to rise and there is a rush to buy it, it is a feeding frenzy.

> *After the announcement of the new product from Widgets Inc., there was a feeding frenzy for its stock.*

fidelity bond (fih-DEL-ih-te bond): A type of insurance that protects a company against dishonesty by its employees.

> *The advantage of a fidelity bond is that not only are we covered against employee theft, but the insurance company will also help us work to prevent it.*

fiduciary (fi-DU-she-ah-re): A person or organization placed in charge of handling assets of another.

> *As executor of his father's will, Alex was the fiduciary responsible for disbursing his father's assets.*

field (feeld): On a computer screen, a field is a separate area where adjacent characters are together.

> *In the field where it says "Name," put your name.*

field staff (feeld staf): People who work for a company but do not work in the home office.

> *The word from our field staff is that customers don't like our new widget products.*

field theory of motivation (feeld THE-o-re of mo-tiv-A-shun): A theory that states motivation of an employee is dependent upon the entire corporate culture.

All the recent downsizing has destroyed motivation for many people. The field theory of motivation shows how difficult it is for an individual to be motivated in an atmosphere such as this.

file (file): A collection of stored data on a computer.

Call up the file on last month's sales and let me know how we did in South America.

file transport protocol (FTP) (file TRANS-port PRO-to-kul): The way files are transferred from one computer to another.

I have an FTP file on the Internet that you can get just by clicking on it.

filing status (FILE-ing STAH-tus): A category, for tax purposes, that you put yourself into. You can be 1) Single Individual, 2) Head of Household, 3) Married filing jointly, 4) Married filing separately.

My filing status is as a single individual.

filtering down (FIL-ter-ing down): The process in which a residential area attracts lower-income people.

The neighborhood near the old baseball stadium is undergoing a filtering down now that there is a brand-new stadium on the other side of the city.

final assembly (fi-NUL as-SEM-ble): Finishing putting a product together—the final steps.

The plant manager showed the visitor around. "This is where we do final assembly," said the plant manager.

finance charge (fi-NANS charj): Any cost associated with receiving credit.

This credit card has a high finance charge.

finance company (fi-NANS KUM-pah-ne): A company that makes loans.

I received a loan from a finance company when I bought a used car.

financial advertising (fi-NAN-shul AD-ver-tize-ing): Advertising aimed at players in the world of finance.

To promote our new mutual fund, we did some financial advertising in the consumer publications.

financial institution (fi-NAN-shul in-stih-TU-shun): An institution that collects money to invest, offers interest for deposits, and makes loans.

My money is in a reputable financial institution and I feel very secure.

financial intermediary (fi-NAN-shul in-ter-ME-de-ah-re): A bank or other financial instititution that smooths the flow of money between those who want to invest it and those who need a loan.

The local bank is the financial intermediary between the big businesses in the city that invest in the bank, and the startup businesses that want its loans.

financial market (fi-NAN-shul MARK-et): A market where financial commodities are traded. There are many different financial markets.

The financial market for stock is the stock market.

financial position (fi-NAN-shul po-ZISH-un): The condition of a firm's financial health in terms of assets, loans, and debts.

Widgets Inc. is in a strong financial position.

financial statement (fi-NAN-shul STATE-ment): A written summary of the financial status of an individual or company, including a balance sheet and income statement.

If you look at the most recent financial statement for Widgets Inc., you will see that this is a solid company.

financial structure (fi-NAN-shul STRUK-chure): The way that a company finances all of its assets. This includes long-term mortgages as well as short-term loans.

The bank looked at our financial structure before deciding to give us a loan.

financing (fi-NANS-ing): To supply money.

We need financing for our new factory.

finder's fee (FINDE-ers fe): A fee paid to an individual for bringing a customer to a supplier of some service or product.

After I signed up for time-sharing I was told I would get a finder's fee if any of my friends signed up.

finished goods (FIN-ishd goods): Products that have been completely put together and are ready for use.

Our widgets are ready to use. We make finished goods.

firm (firm): A nonincorporated company.

Mary went to work for a small law firm in town.

firm offer (firm OFF-er): A written offer that cannot be revoked during a set time period.

There is a firm offer on the table for you to come in as advertising director. The offer's good for this weekend. Let me know by Monday.

firm quote (firm kwote): A specific number offered for a service or product. Not a ballpark figure.

> *"That is a firm quote to fix your exhaust system," said the man at The Muffler Shop.*

first in, first out (FIFO) (first in, first out): A method of recording the value of inventory by asssuming items are sold in the order that they are made.

> *We use the FIFO method of inventory when there is high inflation because it freezes in old costs on items sold. It makes our profit line look better.*

fiscal agent (FIS-kul A-jent): A financial company, often a bank or trust company, that deals with disbursing dividends, redeeming bonds, and paying rents.

> *You have to talk to your fiscal agent about your late dividend check.*

fiscal year (FIS-kul year): An accounting period of any twelve-month period.

> *The company's profits were way down in the last fiscal year.*

Fisher effect (FISH-er ef-FEKT): The relationship between interest rates and inflation rates.

> *The Fisher effect shows that interest rates are a reflection of expected inflation rates.*

fixed cost (fixd kost): A cost that stays the same no matter how much sales go up or down.

> *Our biggest fixed cost is salaries.*

fixed-rate loan (fixd rate lone): A loan that locks in a specific interest rate for the length of the loan.

Jerry doesn't want to get a variable-rate loan and have to worry about the economy, so he got a fixed-rate loan. Now he knows what he owes every month.

flagship (FLAG-ship): An office or product that is most associated with a company because it is the best, the biggest, or the first.

The original handyman's widget is our flagship product. When people think of Widgets Inc., they think of that handyman's widget.

flash report (flash re-PORT): A quick summary of key information that can let a manager make adjustments.

I want a flash report on the production line so I can see if I can figure out why it is going so slow.

flat rate (flat rate): A set cost per unit that doesn't change even if the volume of the order does.

We charge a flat rate for our widgets. Some of our bigger customers don't like this, but many customers appreciate we are trying to offer the lowest possible price all the time.

flat tax (flat tax): A proposed way of charging income tax. Instead of the current progressive system in which the rich pay a higher percentage of their earnings in tax than the poor, a flat tax would call for everyone to pay the same percentage of earnings in taxes.

Many people favor a flat tax because they think it would be the fairest way for everyone.

flexible budget (FLEX-ih-bl BUDJ-et): Various projections of revenues and expenses for various outputs of production.

The president said he wanted to be prepared for whatever happens in sales, so he wanted a flexible budget drawn up.

flexible manufacturing (FLEX-ih-bl man-u-FAK-chure-ing): The ability of manufacturing to transform machines to do many different tasks.

> *We sell widgets for kids and widgets for adults. It's a good thing our factory is capable of flexible manufacturing.*

flextime (FLEX-time): A work schedule in which an employee can start and end the day when he wants, as long as the minimum hours are worked.

> *Now that my kids are in school, it's nice to have flextime so I can go in later on school days.*

float (flote): When a check is on its way from one bank to another.

> *The check for the project I finished hasn't cleared yet. It's still floating.*

floating debt (FLOTE-ing det): A short-term loan that is continually renewed.

> *The company has a floating debt on its new building.*

floating-rate note (FLOTE-ing rate note): A debt instrument for which the rate of interest is adjusted on a set schedule. The rates are tied to Treasury note bills.

> *We have a floating-rate note for the purchase of our new fleet of vehicles.*

floating securities (FLOTE-ing seh-KU-rih-tees): Securities that will be quickly resold in the hope of making a fast profit.

> *I talked to my broker and he's helping me find some floating securities.*

floodplain (flud plane): An area that is subject to regular flooding.

> *If you want to build in the floodplain, your building should be on stilts.*

floor plan (floor plan): The way a building is divided into rooms.

John was not happy with the floor plan of the new building. His office didn't even have windows!

floppy disk (FLOP-pe disk): A medium for storing computer information that pops in and out of a drive in the computer.

I can put that report on a floppy disk and mail it to you.

flowchart (flo chart): A diagram that displays with words, symbols, and arrows how a process works.

Before we redesign how we manufacture widgets, I'd like to see a flowchart of how your changes will speed up the process.

fluctuation (fluk-chu-A-shun): The rise and fall of prices or interest rates.

I don't know if this is a good time to buy stock in Widgets Inc. or not. There has been a real fluctuation in prices lately.

fly-by-night (fli bi nite): A business of questionable character that operates from a post office box and cannot be easily located if there are problems.

My grandmother gave her credit card number to some fly-by-night group passing itself off as a charity.

follow-up letter (FOL-lo up LET-ter): A letter sent to someone who has made an inquiry, providing the inquirer with information requested and, usually, a sales pitch.

Jack asked his secretary to send a follow-up letter to the president of Widgetworld, who called asking about the new widget products being developed by Widgets Inc.

Food and Drug Administration (FDA) (food and drug ad-minis-TRA-shun): Federal agency that regulates the safety of food and pharmaceutical products.

> *Miracles Corporation is waiting for FDA approval for its new diet drug.*

footer (FOOT-er): Something printed in the bottom margin of a document. It appears on every page and can include text, page number, or a graphic.

> *The company wants the pages numbered in the footer of the report.*

footnote (foot note): Data that explains financial statements. Footnotes are essential information that helps the reader understand the company.

> *If you read the footnote about legal costs you will see that we have spent $100,000 fighting two suits, and the rest of our costs are minimal. Our legal bills are not normally so high.*

forced sale (forsd sale): A sale that must be made quickly without searching for a buyer who will pay a fair price. A forced sale is one done under duress, such as a sale in bankruptcy.

> *The bank thought John received way too little for his last business that he sold, but then he explained it was a forced sale.*

forecasting (FOR-kast-ing): Predicting future economic trends.

> *"If I was any good at forecasting, do you think I'd be working here?" said the man on the widgets assembly line.*

foreclosure (for-KLO-zhur): The procedure in which mortgaged property is given legally to the mortgagee because the mortgage has not been paid.

> *The Smiths were worried after John lost his job that they would have no money to pay their mortgage and their house would go into foreclosure.*

foreign culture (FOR-in KUL-chure): The customs of another land that are often important for business people to learn before doing overseas business.

> *If you want to do business overseas, you must learn the foreign cultures of the places where you want to do business. They will help you to be accepted and hopefully prevent a social blunder.*

foreign exchange (FOR-in ex-chanje): Trading money between one country and another.

> *If we are going to do business on the island nation Paradise, we are going to have to find out the foreign exchange rate between dollars and that country's currency, the wooden shebango.*

foreign investment (FOR-in in-VEST-ment): Money that is invested in a country by citizens of another country.

> *The island of Paradise has many new hotels and developments. There has been a lot of foreign investment there.*

forfeiture (FOR-fei-chure): When property is taken by the government for failure to obey a law.

> *The drug dealer lost his house by forfeiture.*

formatting (FOR-mat-ing): Preparing a computer disk for use.

> *I bought a new box of disks and I am formatting them now so I won't have to later.*

formula investing (FOR-mu-la in-VEST-ing): A predetermined strategy for investing that removes spontaneous decisions.

> *All of my investing is formula investing. I know what I am doing and I am not caught up in the latest thing.*

fortuitous loss (for-TU-ih-tous loss): An insurance term about loss that occurs by accident or by chance, rather than an intentional loss.

> *Arson is not considered a fortuitous loss.*

486 processor (486 PROSS-ess-ur): A computer chip model manufactured by Intel.

My computer has a 486 processor and it's plenty fast enough for me.

fractional share (FRAK-shun-ul shar): A unit of stock less than one full share that is created when a company declares a percentage dividend and a stockholder ends up with a percentage of a share.

When you own a fractional share you can either sell its value or pay to upgrade it to a full share.

franchise (FRAN-chise): A license sold to a business or person that allows an operation to use the company's name, product, and promotion.

Frank wants to buy a McDonald's franchise.

fraud (fraud): Intentional deception that causes harm to a person or company.

Those developers doctored the loan documents and stole more than $1 million. That was fraud.

fraudulent misrepresentation (FRAUD-u-lent mis-REP-re-zen-TA-shun): Making a false statement to an insurance company to cause the company to insure a person when it, with proper information, normally would not.

If you have served time in jail for vehicular homicide, it is fraudulent misrepresentation to tell an insurance company that you have a clean driving record.

free and clear (fre and klear): A term for property without liens, mortgages, or restrictions.

Widgets Inc. bought a building from a bankrupt company. Widgets Inc. paid cash for the building and paid off a lien on the property, and then Widgets Inc. owned the property free and clear.

free and open market (fre and open MARK-et): A market where prices and supply are not regulated.

> *The president of Widgets Inc. believes if widgets were traded on a free and open market without having to deal with tariffs, his widgets would sell better overseas.*

Freedom of Information Act (FOIA) (fre-dum of in-for-MA-shun akt): Federal law stating that government documents, unless specifically exempted, must be made available to the public upon request.

> *Journalists often use the Freedom of Information Act to get access to government documents.*

free enterprise (fre EN-ter-prize): Business conducted by the laws of supply and demand without interference from the government.

> *The president of Widgets Inc. named his yacht* Free Enterprise *because his company made the best widgets at the lowest cost. In the free enterprise system his company ruled the widget market.*

free lunch (fre lunch): Something of value that you get for free.

> *The president of Stuff Company, if he had a yacht, would have tried to name it* Free Lunch. *But there is no free lunch. Stuff Company thought it would be easy to take over the widget market. But they didn't make good widgets. They didn't put in the work; thus, they didn't get much of the widget market.*

free-market capitalism (fre MARK-et KAP-ih-tul-ism): An unrestricted, competitive economic system in which there is not government interference or one overwhelming company that dictates the market.

> *You cannot say the automobile industry is free-market capitalism because only a few companies dominate the market.*

free on board (FOB) (fre on bord): A cost for shipping goods. It means that an item is free if picked up at the seller's warehouse, but if it is shipped, there is an extra cost.

> *Our widgets are FOB at our Akron warehouse, meaning if you want them shipped from Akron, you will pay delivery charges.*

free-rein leadership (fre rain LEDE-er-ship): An open system of management in which communication is a high priority and that gives employees the freedom to work hard in their own style.

> *The startup company, Crazy Kids With Ideas, is run by free -rein leadership and it is getting tremendous output from their employees. One employee said, "They showed faith in me and my ideas so I work extra hard."*

frequency (FRE-kwen-se): The number of times an advertisement is in a specific medium for a set time.

> *The holidays are coming up so Widgets Inc. wants to increase the frequency of their ad that has been running every two weeks in* Widgetworld Daily News. *They want the ad to run every day now.*

frequently asked questions (FAQ) (FRE-kwet-le askd KWES-chuns): On the Internet, if you call up a subject, you may find a heading, "FAQ." These are questions the designer of the Web page anticipates getting asked, or has already been asked. FAQ is a good place to learn.

> *If you go to the Web page of the fan club of movie star Guy Smiley, and click on FAQ, you will see his real name and his birthday.*

front-end load (frunt end LODE): An investment fee that is charged at the time of purchase of the investment.

> *Erin likes the Hercules mutual fund, but she doesn't like the idea of paying a front-end load.*

front money (frunt MUN-e): Money needed to start a project.

If we are going to get this new advertising campaign started, we need front money to reserve air time and to give an advance to the advertising agency.

front office (frunt OFF-fis): Where the executives of a company work. The offices of executives are often clustered near the front of the building.

If you want to take a sales trip to Tahiti, you are going to have to check with somebody in the front office.

frozen account (FRO-zen uh-COUNT): A bank account that cannot be accessed. Accounts are frozen by courts because of liens that have not been paid, or in the case of a dispute over who owns the money in the account.

When John and Mary went through their bitter divorce, their bank accounts were frozen until a judge could decide ownership.

fulfillment (ful-FILL-ment): The processsing, filling, and billing of orders that come from direct marketing.

We are going to run an infomercial on late-night television about our new widgets, and we need to hire a fulfillment company or figure a way to process orders ourselves.

full disclosure (full dis-KLO-zhur): Federal requirement that certain relevant information must be revealed about a company to stockholders and potential investors.

Widgets Inc. wanted to hide the consumer group lawsuit from their stockholders, but the company was required by full disclosure to reveal it.

full employment (full em-PLOY-ment): A government estimate of the percentage of people who would be unemployed even if the economy were robust and there were plenty of available jobs.

According to the government, full employment would mean only 4 percent of potential workers are unemployed.

full-service broker (full SERV-is BROK-er): A broker who offers advice in addition to completing trades.

My broker, Harold Finch, is a full-service broker. He advised me to invest in Widgets Inc., and I do not regret following his advice.

full vesting (full VEST-ing): The right to full pension benefits because of longevity even if the person is not employed by the company at the time of retirement.

John worked at Widgets Inc. for twenty-five years, and then he worked at Stuff Company for ten years before retiring. When he retired, he had full vesting from Widgets Inc. Employees get full vesting after twenty years of service.

fully amortized loan (FUL-le ah-MOR-tized lone): A loan that requires payments of principal interest that will pay off the loan in full at the end of its term.

My mortgage is a fully amortized loan.

fully paid policy (FUL-le pade POL-ih-se): A whole-life insurance policy that is paid in full in a set number of payments.

When Mr. Reaper makes thirty payments, his will be a fully paid policy. He will not have to make any more payments and he is insured for the rest of his life.

functional authority (FUNK-shun-ul aw-THOR-ih-te): Responsibility for a task in the hands of the person performing the task.

It's a lot different working at Widgets Inc. than at Stuff Company. Here I have functional authority. I am allowed to make decisions on the spot.

functional organization (FUNK-shun-ul OR-gan-i-ZA-shun): An organization in which departments are created along functional lines.

> *Widgets Inc. is a functional organization. It includes the marketing department, accounting, personnel, and administration.*

function key (FUNK-chun ke): Set of keys on a computer keyboard, usually F1 through F10. These keys take on different utilities depending on the software being run.

> *If you want to run that new program from Smartypants Software, you should learn how to use each function key.*

funding (FUND-ing): Providing money to pay for a project.

> *I think we should provide funding to widget development. The potential of the new widget technology is amazing, but it still needs to be developed.*

fund manager (fund MAN-eh-jer): The investment company that manages a mutual fund.

> *The Hercules fund is run by a respected fund manager.*

fund-raising (FUND-raze-ing): Soliciting contributions for nonprofit organizations.

> *Jonathan Widget is involved in fund-raising for the environmental group, Save the Chipmunks.*

fungibles (FUN-jih-bls): Goods in which any unit can be replaced by another unit of the same thing.

> *Dollar bills are fungibles. One is as good as another.*

futures contract (FU-chures KON-trakt): An agreement to buy or sell a certain amount of a certain commodity on or by a specfic date.

> *Elmer the Popcorn King has a futures contract to purchase the fall harvest of corn from Big Faceless Farm Company.*

gain (GANE): Extra money received over the book value of an item.

We sold the antique widgets to a collector and realized a nice gain.

gain sharing (gane SHAR-ing): A method of motivating employees with cash or stock. The bonus is tied to some performance level that must be reached by a group, and then the compensation is shared by all in the group.

I like the gain-sharing program at Widgets Inc. If we meet our sales goal, we receive $5,000 each.

gaming (GAME-ing): A simulation of a competitive situation between two or more participants. In such a situation, only one wins at the expense of the others. The idea is to find parameters for success in real-life situations.

We are doing some internal gaming on the Peterson bid to try to figure out the best strategy.

garnish (GAR-nish): To take part of an employee's wages and turn it over to a person who has won a court settlement against that person.

Ralph was jailed for refusing to pay child support, but the judge released him after Ralph agreed to have his wages garnished for the next fifteen years.

gender analysis (JEN-der ah-NAL-ih-sis): Studying mailing lists to determine the gender of each name on the list. Direct-mail pitches are then geared toward that particular gender. However, some mistakes will occur since some names are common for both genders.

Widgets Inc. bought a mailing list and immediately ordered a gender analysis of it. Most of the company's products are for men, but it recently came out with a new widget for women and it wants to market that product mostly to females.

General Accounting Office (GAO) (JEN-er-ul uh-COUNT-ing OFF-iss): Federal office that oversees the financial transactions of all federal agencies and that reports directly to Congress.

The GAO is auditing the contract between Widgets Inc. and the Department of Education.

General Agreement on Tariffs and Trade (GATT) (JEN-er-ul ah-GRE-ment on TAR-ifs and trade): International agreement to encourage trade by reducing barriers such as tariffs.

Some people say that GATT is good because it has opened up markets for American products, but others think it has made it easier for companies to move jobs overseas.

general expense (JEN-er-ul es-PENS): An expense in operations that does not come from sales, administration, or materials.

Our utility bills are a general expense.

general fund (JEN-er-ul fund): The operating account of a government agency.

Money in the general fund is used to pay utility bills.

general ledger (JEN-er-ul LEDJ-er): A formal record of all of a business's accounts.

The president of the company studied the general ledger, trying to figure a way to cut costs and raise profits.

general liability insurance (JEN-er-ul li-ah-BIL-ih-te in-SHURE-ens): Insurance coverage if anyone is injured using your product or while on your premises.

An old lady slipped and fell on our sidewalk, but we have general liability insurance so we are covered.

general lien (JEN-er-ul leen): A lien on all the property owned by a debtor.

Consumers won a lawsuit against Stuff Company and a judge placed a general lien on all holdings by Stuff Company.

Generally Accepted Accounting Principles (GAAP) (JEN-er-ul-le ak-SEPT-ed uh-COUNT-ing PRIN-sih-pls): The rules and standards accountants follow in recording transactions and making financial statements. The principles include broad guidelines and specific instructions.

Our last accountant was so incompetent that he not only didn't follow GAAP, he didn't really even know them.

general partner (JEN-er-ul PART-ner): A partner who has a say in how a company is run and is also liable for actions of the company.

Stan brought Sue in as a general partner because he needed the investment money and because he wanted Sue to help him run the business.

general price index (JEN-er-ul price IN-dex): There are a number of general price indexes, which measure the change in prices of a broad category of products or services.

One general price index is the Consumer Price Index, which measures the cost of a number of items that consumers often buy.

general strike (JEN-er-ul strike): A well-coordinated large-scale work stoppage by most of the workers designed to apply pressure to a company or government to get it to go along with union demands.

Workers on the island nation of Paradise called for a general strike to begin on Wednesday if the government does not pass laws for a safer workplace.

generic (jeh-NER-ik): The entire category of a product, as opposed to a specific brand.

My kids don't need a fancy widget by Widgets Inc. They will be quite happy with a generic widget. Heck, they're all the same anyway.

genetic engineering (jeh-NET-ik en-jih-NEER-ing): The altering of DNA to make specific changes in future generations of a plant or animal.

Scientists have used genetic engineering to breed large, tasty tomatoes.

gentrification (JEN-trih-fih-KA-shun): When an older, poor neighborhood is revitalized by an infusion of money and new residents, causing the poorer residents to leave.

The last decade of gentrification downtown has transformed the area.

gift tax (gift tax): A tax on gifts received over a certain amount in a set period.

Sue's parents sent her $5,000 on three different occasions last year. She knows she owes a gift tax on part of the money.

gigabyte (GIG-ah-bite): A billion bytes of information.

My new computer has a gigabyte of storage space on the hard drive.

gilt-edged security (gilt edjd seh-KU-rih-te): A dependably successful bond that has earned consistent profits to cover interest.

Bonds issued by the island of Paradise are gilt-edged securities.

global hedging (GLO-bel HEDJ-ing): A way of managing risk by balancing different business units.

Widgets Inc. did some global hedging by offering low-end doohickeys and high-end thingamajigs.

global market (GLO-bel MARK-et): The way that all markets around the world affect one another. As one market closes, another opens and what happens in one has a bearing on action in another.

A company can no longer just concentrate on the U.S. There is a global market that is integrated.

glut (glut): An oversupply of a product that makes selling all of the product at a regular price impossible.

Two huge orders were canceled after the widgets were already produced. There is now a glut of widgets. We need to cut prices to reduce inventory.

goal (gole): A specific objective to be achieved within a specific time period.

We have a goal of selling more widgets this year than we did last year.

going private (GO-ing PRI-vet): Transformation of a company from public to private. This can happen if the company repurchases its shares, or if an outside investor purchases all the shares.

The grandchildren of Jonathan Widget have purchased all the stock in Widgets Inc. The company is going private.

going public (GO-ing PUB-lik): The first offering of shares of a private company to the public. When a company goes public, it gets an infusion of money, and also new regulations it must follow.

Stuff Company is going public in a month to raise funds for its overseas push.

golden handcuffs (GOLD-en HAND-kufs): A means of keeping key employees in a company through stock options. Employees in this situation cannot afford to leave.

Emily, the techno wiz, wanted to leave Widgets Inc., but she was tied there with a set of golden handcuffs that made her a millionaire for staying.

golden handshake (GOLD-en HAND-shake): Incentives for early retirement.

Alfred decided to accept the golden handshake offered by his employer. The offer was too good to turn down, and besides, he wanted to spend time with his grandchildren.

golden parachute (GOLD-en PAR-ah-chute): A special deal for an executive that guarantees if the person retires or the company is bought out, the executive will receive a sweet package of benefits such as stock options and severance pay.

Before Amy took a job with Widgets Inc., she insisted on a golden parachute because she had heard rumors the company could be bought out.

gold standard (golde STAND-erd): A way of valuing currency in which money is worth a specific amount of gold. The U.S. stopped using the gold standard in 1933.

Some politicians think putting the U.S. back on the gold standard would help the economy.

goods (goods): Things that are bought and sold that are not real estate or investments.

The price of goods from Widgets Inc. has gone up because the cost of supplies has gone up.

goods and services (goods and SERV-is-s): The output of an economy. Goods are items and services are things people do for others.

Widgets Inc. offers a wide array of goods and services.

goodwill (good will): An intangible asset a business accumulates by doing the right thing for its customers and suppliers, and by being active in its community and in charities.

Widgets Inc. built up some goodwill by being active in the Save the Chipmunks campaign.

grace period (grase PE-re-ud): The amount of time after a payment is due on a loan or an insurance policy that most companies will grant customers before default on the loan or cancellation of the policy occurs.

After Frank was laid off from his job, he missed his insurance payment but he managed to land enough odd jobs to make the payment before the grace period was up.

graduated wage (GRAD-u-a-ted waje): Salary structure in which employees receive incremental raises based on seniority and promotions.

Sally was happy to get an entry-level position at Widgets Inc. because she knew the company offered a graduated-wage structure and within a few years she would be earning much more.

grandfather clause (GRAND-fah-ther klaws): A provision in a new rule that exempts those who are already engaged in an activity from coming under regulation.

The new zoning regulation increasing lot sizes in new developments does not affect our lot because it falls under the grandfather clause.

grant (grant): A donation of money from a government or private foundation toward a project that is thought to be beneficial to the public.

Widgets Inc. supports a foundation that gives out grants to struggling artists.

Graphical User Interface (GUI) (GRAF-ik-ul USE-er IN-ter-face): A way of communicating with a computer in which the screen has pictures (icons) on it that stand for commands. Click on the picture and the command is executed.

Andy never wanted a computer but when he saw how easy it is to use GUI, he decided to get one.

graphics interchange format (GIF) (GRAF-iks in-ter-chanje FOR-mat): A popular type of computer file for storing pictures. In order to view a GIF file, you need a GIF viewer.

Widgets Inc. put some pictures of its new products in a GIF file for potential customers to download.

graveyard shift (GRAVE-yard shift): An overnight workshift that usually begins at midnight and ends at 8 A.M.

Carlos took a second job working the graveyard shift.

Great Depression (grate de-PREH-shun): The period of the worst economic downturn in U.S. history, from 1929 until the beginnning of World War II. Millions were unemployed, companies closed, and stocks plummeted.

Jonathan Widget's son, Edgar, grew up a rich boy during the Great Depression and never experienced how hard those times were for others.

green card (grene kard): A registration card for legal immigrants.

The first thing Max did after moving to the U.S. from the island country of Paradise was apply for his green card so he could work here.

gross (grose): An undivided amount.

The president of the company wants the figure for gross sales last month.

Gross Domestic Product (GDP) (grose do-MES-tik PROD-ukt): The total value of goods and services produced by a country in a given year.

The president was happy with this year's high GDP, especially because this is an election year.

gross earnings (grose URN-ings): How much an employee earns before taxes, Social Security, and employee benefits are taken out.

Susan is happy with her gross earnings, but after everything is taken out of her paycheck she barely has enough to get by.

gross estate (grose es-TATE): The total value of a person's estate before taxes and debts are collected.

Jonathan Widget's gross estate included all the stock of Widgets Inc., five mansions, and a high-rise in Manhattan.

gross profit (grose PROF-it): The value of revenues minus costs.

The revenue for that order of widgets was $50,000 and the cost to make them was $30,000. The gross profit on that order was $20,000.

gross receipts (grose re-SETES): The total sales in one year without any allowance for returned merchandise.

Our gross receipts for this year were our highest ever, but that doesn't tell the whole story because we also had the highest number of returns ever.

gross revenue (grose REV-eh-nu): Total sales without allowances for discounts or returns.

If potential investors only looked at gross revenue, they would think Widgets Inc. had an even better year than it did. But the figure did not include all the discounts given to induce customers to buy large quantities.

ground lease (ground lese): A lease on a piece of land only.

Widgets Inc. has a forty-year ground lease on the spot where it will build its new skyscraper.

group interview (group IN-ter-vu): An interview of a group of people about a specific situation. Or . . . The interview of an individual by a group of people.

> *The company conducted a group interview with those in produc-*
> *tion about problems on that line. Or . . . Before Al was hired as an*
> *accountant by Widgets Inc., he went through a group interview with*
> *someone from human resources, the president of the company, and*
> *the head of accounting.*

growth fund (grothe fund): A mutual fund that offers a chance for long-term growth but also greater risk than more conservative funds.

> *Amy put half of her money into bank accounts or conservative*
> *funds, but she invested the other half in a growth fund. She is hoping*
> *the growth fund will increase fast enough to fund college for her*
> *three boys.*

growth rate (grothe rate): The percentage change in a specific financial characteristic of a company.

> *The growth rate of dividends for Widgets Inc. stock has gone up*
> *dramatically since the company introduced its new products last*
> *year. Before that, the stock had grown at a steady pace with its old*
> *reliable widgets, but the new widgets caused such a stir that the rate*
> *of growth in the last year has skyrocketed.*

guarantee (gar-en-TEE): A promise that a product will work as directed. If the product does not, the company promises to replace it or reimburse the customer.

> *The new widgets come with a lifetime guarantee.*

guarantor (GAR-en-tor): A person who guarantees the payment of a debt that is owed by somone else.

> *Jim's mother is the guarantor of the loan for his new Corvette.*

guardian deed (gard-e-en dede): When real estate is sold by someone who is not capable of administering his own affairs, the deed is given by a guardian charged with administering the personal affairs of that person. That is a guardian deed.

After Ralph suffered his debilitating stroke, his daughter Heidi was appointed guardian of his affairs. When his house was sold, she gave a guardian deed to the buyer.

guide (gide): A document describing practices and procedures to be followed in sequence for the success of some operation.

If you want to know how to run the software, you should read the guide first.

guild (gild): An organization similiar to a union in which the consensus views of the group are represented.

The Writers Guild picketed Widgetworld *magazine because of the low prices paid for articles.*

habeas corpus (HA-be-us KOR-pus): A legal procedure to get a ruling on whether someone held in custody is being held legally.

The accused stockbroker filed a writ of habeas corpus so he could have a hearing before a judge on whether he should be held in jail.

half-life (haf life): How long it takes to pay off half the principal of a mortgage-backed security.

This security has a half-life of fifteen years.

halo effect (HA-lo ef-FEKT): The vibes, negative or positive, that a particular characteristic gives to a person.

Thorton's grandfather was Jonathan Widget, founder of this huge company. That gives him an instant halo effect whenever he meets anyone in the company.

hammering the market (HAM-mer-ing the MARK-et): Selling a large number of stocks in anticipation of an economic downturn.

Some big investors in high-tech have been hammering the market lately, causing some analysts to wonder if high-tech is due for a downturn.

hard copy (hard KOP-e): A printout on paper.

I will send you a computer disk with that report on it, and I will also send hard copy.

hard-core unemployed (hard kor un-em-PLOYD): A category of people including those who have not worked in a long time, and those who have never worked.

No matter what economic policies the country adopts, there will always be one segment of hard-core unemployed.

hard currency (hard KUR-ren-se): Currency from stable nations that is accepted internationally as reliably holding value.

The U.S. dollar is hard currency, while the wooden shebango from the island of Paradise is not.

hard disk (hard disk): An internal storage medium in a computer. A hard disk, unlike a floppy disk, is built into a computer and it usually holds huge amounts of information.

Susie Wordsmith, the novelist, has all twenty-five of her novels, and many different drafts, stored on her hard drive.

hard goods (hard goods): Durable merchandise.

Televisions, toasters, and wheelbarrows are hard goods.

hardship (HARD-ship): A demonstrated financial need that allows a person to withdraw funds from a 401K plan.

Alfred needs money to pay for his daughter's college tuition, so he put in a hardship claim to get money from his 401K.

hardware (HARD-ware): The electronic and mechanical parts that make up a computer.

I think the problem with my computer is in the hardware, either the hard drive or the CPU.

hatchet man (HATCH-et): The person in charge of telling people their employment at a company is terminated.

Stan has been a bundle of nerves while the company is downsizing because he is the designated hatchet man.

header (HED-er): Something printed in the top margin of a document. It can include text, page number, or a graphic.

We always have the company logo in the header of all of our documents.

headhunter (HEAD-HUNT-er): An executive search firm.

Mary wasn't looking for a new job but she was contacted by a headhunter, so she agreed to listen to offers.

headquarters (HEAD-KWAR-ters): The home office of a company.

Frank is leaving for a week for a big meeting at headquarters.

hearsay (HEAR-say): Statement made by one person in a company about another that may or may not be true. Hearsay is rumor rather than direct fact.

Jack told me that Andy said that George isn't working hard anymore, but it is just hearsay. George's performance has been fine.

heavy industry (HEV-e IN-dus-tre): Big production industries such as steel, autos, and petroleum. These industries require lots of raw materials and employ large amounts of people.

> *Environmentalists are often citing heavy industry for being insensitive to the environment.*

hedge (hedg): A way of trying to reduce risk in business or investment.

> *We are going into the widget business, but just as a hedge we are not stopping making dohickeys.*

hemline theory (HEM-line THE-o-re): A half-serious theory that the market rises and falls with the fashion of hemlines. The higher the hemline, goes the theory, the stronger the market.

> *The hemline theory received great fanfare in the 1960s when hemlines went up and so did the market.*

hiccup (HIK-kup): An unusual turn in the market that is corrected within days.

> *The market has grown steadily for a year except for a hiccup one day in March when it dropped by 100 points. But that and more was gained back the next day.*

hidden agenda (HID-den ah-jen-dah): A secretive set of objectives held by an individual.

> *You can't trust Smithers. I'm sure he has a hidden agenda but I don't know exactly what.*

hidden asset (HID-den AS-set): An understated value on a balance sheet.

> *Widgets Inc.'s widget-making equipment has a higher value than what is shown on the balance sheet. It is a hidden asset.*

hidden reserve (HID-den re-ZERV): An understatement of net worth.

The Smiths have a hidden reserve in their vast art collection, but when they sell it the value will be converted to cash and no longer be hidden.

hierarchy (HI-er-ar-ke): The pyramid of responsibility within an organization.

The CEO is at the top of the company's hierarchy.

high credit (hi KRED-IT): The highest amount of outstanding loans recorded for a particular customer.

Look at the history of a customer and you will see where they have high credit.

highest and best use (HI-est and best use): A term for the most profitable possible use of a piece of real estate.

Although there is a house on that lot, it is commercially zoned; therefore, the highest and best use for that property would be a commercial development.

high flyer (hi FLI-er): A volatile, high-priced stock that is subject to price fluctuations and is a risky investment.

The stock of Smartypants Software is a high flyer. Some say it will continue to grow at incredible rates, while others are leery that the bottom could fall out at any moment.

high-growth venture (hi grothe VEN-ture): A small company that is set up to grow fast and increase profits rapidly.

Smartypants Software started out as a high-growth venture and it has been successful in meeting its goals.

high-pressure selling (hi PRESS-shure SELL-ing): A pushy selling technique to get a person to buy insurance that they may or may not need.

> *I was going to use Slick Insurance but the agent kept coming at me with such high-pressure selling that it turned me off.*

high (hi): When a stock hits its highest value compared to any previous prices for the past year.

> *Widgets Inc. stock hit a new high yesterday.*

high technology (hi tek-NOL-o-je): A term, often associated with computers, that is a category of very new, innovative technology.

> *Widgets Inc. is not a high-technology company, but it uses high technology in its daily operations.*

hit list (hit list): A list of potential financial backers or of potential customers.

> *The sales manager asked everyone on the sales staff to provide him with a hit list they would approach in the next month.*

hit the bricks (hit the briks): The action of going on strike.

> *The union president warned us to be prepared to hit the bricks if the company did not accept the latest contract offer from our union.*

holding (HOLD-ing): Property that a person owns through possession of the title.

> *Edgar Widget, majority owner in Widgets Inc., lists four mansions among his holdings.*

holding company (HOLD-ing KUM-pah-ne): A corporation that owns stock and manages more than one company.

In addition to being the top producer of widgets in the world, Widgets Inc. is a holding company for its many subsidiaries.

holding period (HOLD-ing PEH-re-ud): The amount of time an investment is expected to be owned.

The holding period for a five-year CD is five years.

holdout (HOLD-out): A person who wants to get more money in a negotiation and refuses to come to an early agreement.

We have most of our management team in place for the new company but the person we have targeted to run marketing is a holdout.

home office (home OFF-fis): An office that a person has set up in her house.

After Gwen was downsized from Widgets Inc., she set up a widget consulting business and operated out of a home office.

home office deduction (home OFF-fis de-DUK-shun): The tax deduction allowed for a home office that is used exclusively for business.

My accountant told me to keep track of all of my utilities costs because I would be able to use a percentage of them in my home office deduction.

home-owner equity account (HOMEone-er): A second mortgage given to home owners that allow them to tap into equity built up in the property.

The Smiths used their home-owner equity account to build an addition on their house.

home page (home paje): A page on the World Wide Web that individuals or businesses set up to tell about themselves.

Widgets Inc. has designed a home page with graphics of all of its recent widget innovations.

honorarium (hon-o-RAr-e-um): The fee a professional receives to perform a special service.

Edgar Widget received an honorarium from the Widget Makers Association for a speech he recently gave on the current state of the widget.

Horatio Alger (ho-RA-she-o AL-jer): An author of rags-to-riches moralistic stories.

The tale of Jonathan Widget's rise from the slums of Chicago to the top of a huge company is just like an Horatio Alger story.

horizontal analysis (hor-ih-ZON-tel ah-NAL-ih-sis): An analysis of financial statements that allows for comparison of numbers from one accounting period to another.

Widgets Inc. presented a horizontal analysis of its sales figures from this year and last year so stockholders could see how its new products have increased sales.

horizontal conflict (hor-ih-ZON-tel KON-flikt): Intense competition for the market.

Widgets Inc. and Stuff Company both have retail outlets in my small town, causing horizontal conflict that is hurting both of them as well as smaller competitors.

horizontal integration (hor-ih-ZON-tel in-teh-GRA-shun): The domination of one part of a production process by a company that monopolizes the resources that go into that phase.

Almost every widget company in the world gets their doohickeys, a critical component of widgets, from Tuck Company. Widgets Inc. bought Tuck Company, giving it horizontal integration.

hot issue (hot ISH-u): A new stock that is in great demand and is priced high.

Smartypants Software is a hot issue because it is new and in demand.

house account (house uh-COUNT): An account that is managed from inside a brokerage firm.

The salesman told me that he couldn't help me because the account I want to invest in is a house account. He gave me the number of the firm.

household workers (HOUSE-hold WORK-ers): People who work in a house. Employers of these workers do not have to pay income taxes on them but they are required to pay Social Security.

If you are a politician and you have household workers, be sure to pay Social Security taxes on them or it could ruin your career.

Housing and Urban Development (HUD), Department of (HOUSE-ing and UR-ban de-VEL-up-ment): Government agency in charge of implementing federal housing programs.

The new housing project for handicapped people is a HUD project.

housing starts (HOUSE-ing starts): An economic indicator representing the number of new construction starts on houses in a given period.

Economists say the increase in housing starts in the last two quarters is good news for the economy.

HTML (h-t-m-l): Hypertext Markup Language. These are the rules that govern the way documents are created so they can be read by a WWW browser.

Before I put together my Web page, I had to learn HTML.

HTTP (h-t-t-p): Hypertext Transport Protocol, the protocol used by WWW servers.

If you want to put together a large Web site, you have to understand HTTP.

huckster (HUK-ster): A salesperson who will say almost anything to get a sale.

When we visited Cape Cod we had no intention of buying time-share property but we were talked into it by a slick-talking huckster who told us the property would triple in value in five years.

human approach (HU-men ap-PROCHE): A way of trying to cut insurance costs by convincing people they should live a safer lifestyle.

Antismoking campaigns are part of the human approach used to reduce health-care costs.

human relations (HU-men re-LA-shuns): A theory of management that stresses a human approach to motivating people.

People will work harder if they like their jobs. Giving them a reason besides a paycheck to come to worrk is just part of human relations.

human resources (HU-men re-SORS-es): The people who make up a company.

In any company, the biggest asset you have is human resources.

human resources department (HU-men re-SORS-es de-PART-ment): The department in a company that deals with recruitment, pay, and discharging.

Send your resume to the human resources department and you will be called if they want to interview you.

hush money (hush MUN-e): Money paid to someone to buy their silence on a controversial or illegal activity.

The company offered Janet hush money to be quiet about the environmental mess it has caused, but she refused to be bribed.

hype (hipe): The generating of media excitement about a product.

There was a lot of hype about the new widgets by Widgets Inc.

hyperinflation (HI-per-in-FLA-shun): A period of overwhelming inflation in which currency becomes virtually worthless.

There has been hyperinflation on the island of Paradise where a loaf of bread used to cost two wooden shebangos but now costs 400,000 wooden shebangos.

hyperlink (Hi-per-link): A link in a computer document that brings the user to another document. These links are usually represented by highlighted words or images.

I called up Widgets Inc.'s Web page and on it there was a hyperlink that brought me a history of Jonathan Widget, who founded the company.

IBM-PC (i-b-m-p-c): Microcomputer designed by IBM that has been cloned by many other companies.

Harold owns an IBM-PC and is happy because so much software can run on it.

icon (I-kon): A small picture on a computer screen that represents a command. Click your mouse on the picture and the command is executed.

The icon for my e-mail is a little tiny mailbox.

ideal capacity (i-DE-el kah-PAS-ih-te): The largest possible volume of output if a facility is operating at maximum efficiency with no foul-ups.

We have so many orders for Christmas that I don't think that even if this factory was running at ideal capacity we would be able to fill them all.

idle capacity (I-dl kah-PAS-ih-te): Unused capacity in conjunction with a lack of raw materials or skilled labor.

There is some idle capacity at Widgets Inc. because the labor pool around here is so poor.

idle time (I-dl time): The time when an employee is unable to work because of a breakdown in the machinery required for production.

Joe has had a lot of idle time the past couple of weeks because the new widget press has been breaking down regularly.

illegal dividend (il-LE-gel DIV-ih-dend): A dividend payment that breaks either state laws or the company's charter.

The board of directors voted to pay a dividend from capital surplus, but that is an illegal dividend because it would break the company.

illiquid (il-LIK-wid): Not having enough cash flow to pay debt obligations.

The downturn in the economy has made this company illiquid for two straight quarters.

image advertising (IM-ej AD-ver-tize-ing): Advertising strategy in which a product is presented as exemplifying a particular image such as one of luxury or hipness.

Widgets Inc. went with image advertising when it hired rock star Josie Petunia to tell people how hip it is to own a widget.

impact statement (IM-pakt STATE-ment): A document in which the effects of a proposed project are studied and predicted.

> *When Widgets Inc. wanted to build a plant on the shores of Lake Erie, environmentalists demanded an environmental impact statement be prepared.*

impairment of capital (im-PAIR-ment of KAP-ih-tel): When stated capital has gone down because of dividend payments or other losses.

> *When Widgets Inc. lost a major lawsuit, it suffered an impairment of capital to pay for a portion of damages and for higher insurance premiums.*

impasse (IM-pass): A stop in negotiations because neither side will budge.

> *The union and management at Widgets Inc. have reached an impasse in their negotiations. Both sides agreed it would be best to halt negotiations for a week before trying again.*

imperfect market (im-PER-fekt MARK-et): A market that can be affected by select individual consumers or producers.

> *The widget market is an imperfect market because Widgets Inc. is so big that it has unusual influence on supplies and prices.*

implied warranty (im-PLIDE war-REN-te): A warranty that exists by law but is not written.

> *In my state, there is an implied warranty on used cars for thirty days.*

impound (im-POUND): The legal seizing of merchandise, funds, or records.

> *Sam's car was impounded by the police because he failed to pay taxes on it.*

improvement (im-PROOV-ment): Any new physical change to land or property that increases the value.

After Widgets Inc. bought this old building, the company made a number of improvements to it, including upgrading the heating system, and landscaping.

imputed income (im-PUTE-ed IN-kum): The money a taxpayer saves by performing a service on his own.

A painter who paints his own house has imputed income for that service and he does not have to pay taxes on it.

incentive pay (in-SEN-tiv pay): Bonus pay for producing above a certain level.

The sales department offers incentive pay for every order you receive above your quota.

incentive stock option (in-SEN-tiv stok OP-shun): Compensation plan for employees in which qualifying stock options are not taxed until sold.

One thing Wendy likes about working at Widgets Inc. is the incentive stock option.

income (IN-kum): The amount of money received.

The new widgets are hot sellers and have had a significant impact on the income of Widgets Inc.

income accounts (IN-kum uh-COUNTS): Accounting term for revenue and expense accounts.

By looking at income accounts you will get a good sense of what projects are bringing money in, as well as our biggest costs.

income approach (IN-kum ap-PROCHE): A way of appraising real estate by examining expected annual income from the property.

When you use the income approach on that piece of underutilized commercial property, you will see it is worth a lot more money than you think.

income group (IN-kum group): A demographic group made up of people who have similiar income levels.

Widgets Inc. targeted their new widget to people who make more than $100,000 a year, and so they called it a luxury widget.

income property (IN-kum PROP-er-te): Real estate that is expected to bring in money.

The Smiths own four homes, but rent out three as income property. They plan to sell them in fifteen years when their son is old enough for college, and they expect to make enough to pay his tuition to Harvard.

income realization (IN-kum RE-el-i-ZA-shun): Payment at the time of sale or at the time a service is performed.

My plumber wanted income realization as soon as he fixed my toilet.

income stream (IN-kum streme): A steady flow of money from an investment or a business.

My stock in Widgets Inc. has given me a nice income stream for the past twenty years.

income tax (IN-kum tax): Tax on the income of a person or a business.

You think you are earning good money, but then you look at your pay stub and realize what a huge percentage is going to income taxes.

incompetent (in-KOM-peh-tent): The inability to perform a job.

> *Although Arnold's supervisor likes him personally, he knew that Arnold had to be fired because Arnold is just plain incompetent.*

incorporate (in-KOR-po-rate): To form a corporation.

> *Stuff Company has decided to incorporate in order to give the owners legal protection.*

increased cost endorsement (IN-kresed kost en-DORS-ment): Insurance term for the covering of extra costs in rebuilding a building according to new zoning laws.

> *The old Widgets Inc. factory was on the same site for seventy-five years before it burned down. The company needed an increased cost endorsement for the new construction because new zoning laws required many costly environmental safeguards on all new construction.*

incremental analysis (in-kre-MEN-tel ah-NAL-ih-sis): A decision-making method in which only relevant costs are figured between two alternatives. Costs that are the same, and therefore irrelevant, are dropped in such an analysis.

> *Widgets Inc. did an incremental analysis on whether it is worth-while to buy a new widget press.*

incremental spending (in-kre-MEN-tel SPEND-ing): A way of budgeting for advertising in direct proportion to sales. Spending can either go up or down, depending on sales and strategy.

> *Widgets Inc. has a strategy of incremental spending in which the budget for advertising goes up if sales go down. Stuff Company also has a strategy of incremental spending, but that company drops its advertising budget if sales go down.*

indemnity (in-DEM-nih-te): An obligation by an insurance company to pay for a loss.

The indemnity for the loss of Widgets Inc.'s factory in a fire was held up by legal hassles.

indenture (in-DEN-chure): A formal agreement between a bondholder and an issuer of bonds that states the conditions of the bond.

Read the indenture to see what covenants are in it.

independent adjuster (in-de-PEND-ent ad-JUST-er): A private contractor who works for more than one insurance company, making adjustments to claims.

After my auto accident, an independent adjuster came to look at my car.

index (IN-dex): A statistical reading of economic conditions by putting them in the context of a base year or base month.

One of the most used indexes is the Consumer Price Index.

indirect costs (in-dih-REKT kosts): Costs in manufacturing that are not directly part of product costs. These include electricity, insurance, and taxes.

When Widgets Inc. located its factory in midtown Manhattan it should have realized how high its indirect cost would be for such a location.

indirect labor (in-dih-REKT LA-bur): The costs of paying factory workers who are not directly involved in making products for sale.

The cost of a janitor is indirect labor.

individual bargaining (in-dih-VID-u-el BAR-gun-ing): Negotiations between an individual and company.

> *I liked it better when a union did my negotiating for me. It seems ever since I've been doing individual bargaining, I have been at a disadvantage.*

individualism (in-dih-VID-u-el-ism): A style of work that has strengths and drawbacks. The person who practices such a style does things his own way. This leads to creativity and motivation, but this person may not be a good team player.

> *Widgets Inc. discourages individualism because it wants every employee to think and act alike.*

Individual Retirement Account (IRA) (in-div-VID-u-el re-TIRE-ment uh-COUNT): A trust fund an employee can take out and contribute into up to $2,000 a year for the future.

> *My father told me that since my company does not have a pension plan, I should take out an IRA.*

inductive reasoning (in-DUK-tiv re-ZUN-ing): Taking a small amount of information and trying to reach a logical conclusion about what should be done in that circumstance.

> *The president of Widgets Inc. used inductive reasoning to decide to bring his products into European markets based on the success of his competitor, Stuff Company, in Europe.*

industrial engineer (in-DUS-tre-el en-jih-NEER): A person who studies materials, equipment, and workers and the way they are integrated.

> *Widgets Inc. has hired an industrial engineer to see if the company could be more efficient at making widgets.*

industrial fatigue (in-DUS-tre-el fah-TEGE): Burnout in a factory. Someone who has industrial fatigue is emotionally and physically spent from the job and unable to do his best.

Half the workers in the Widgets Inc. factory are suffering from industrial fatigue because it is a miserable place to work.

industrialist (in-DUS-tre-el-ist): An individual at the top of an industrial business.

Jonathan Widget, founder of the giant company Widgets Inc., was one of the first industrialists.

industrial park (in-DUS-tre-el park): A place zoned for manufacturing and industry.

Widgets Inc. put its newest factory in an industrial park in Denver.

industry (in-DUS-tre): A manufacturing business.

Widgets Inc. is a business in the industry of widgets.

industry ratios (in-DUS-tre RA-she-ose): The median financial ratios for an industry. These are used to compare how a particular company compares to the overall industry.

I want to check out industry ratios to see how our financial ratios compare.

industry standard (in-DUS-tre STAND-erd): A common way of doing things in an industry.

All widgets have a half-inch piece of plastic on the handle. That is the industry standard.

inefficiencies in the market (in-ef-FISH-en-sees in the MARK-et): A failure of investors to recognize the direction of a stock, whether up or down.

> *Despite the best intentions of investors, they did not forsee the drop in price of Widgets Inc. stock. This is an example of inefficiencies in the market.*

inefficient markets (in-ef-FISH-ent MARK-ets): Markets that are not studied.

> *If you want to take a risk with your money, you may find a great opportunity in inefficient markets.*

infant-industry argument (IN-fent in-DUS-tre AR-gu-ment): Argument made by businesses in a new industry that they need protection from foreign competition while they take time to establish themselves.

> *The high-tech widget industry is so new that many companies are making an infant-industry argument for tariffs on foreign competition.*

inferior good (in-FE-re-ur): A product that is demanded less by customers who find their income increasing.

> *Used cars are an inferior good because when a customer's income goes up, he will want to buy a new car.*

inflation (in-FLA-shun): A hike in prices.

> *Politicians are especially worried about inflation during election years because they know voters don't like to see prices rise and often blame incumbent politicians.*

informal leader (in-FORM-ul LEDE-er): A person who gets his authority based on a group's belief and not by any formal position.

> *On the factory floor, everybody respected Shirley Morrison so much that even those in authority recognized her power as an informal leader.*

information age (in-for-MA-shun aje): The latest stage of economic development in which information is the product of utmost importance.

Many say the information age started when computers began connecting to the Internet.

information retrieval (in-for-MA-shun re-TREVE-ul): The use of computer systems to store and retrieve information.

We have a great system of information retrieval because if I want to know anything about the operation of our company I can find it in our computer files.

information return (in-for-MA-shun re-TURN): A document submitted to the Internal Revenue Service that does not compute how much is owed but rather only provides taxpayer information to the IRS.

I filled out my 1099 form, which is an information return.

information superhighway (in-for-MA-shun su-per-HI-way): The various mediums for the electronic transfer of information.

Once you get out on the information superhighway, especially the Internet, you can find out anything.

Information Systems (IS) (in-for-MA-shun SIS-tems): The department in a company that deals with the processing and sharing of information, especially via computer systems.

John from Information Systems is looking at all options for a new computer system at our company.

infrastructure (IN-frah-STRUK-chure): The physical makeup of how a country operates, including its highway system, water system, and communications system.

Many in America say the nation's infrastructure needs to be seriously updated.

infringement (in-FRINJ-ment): Abusing another's protected right.

When Stuff Company introduced new widgets with a logo very similar to that of Widgets Inc., it was clearly a case of copyright infringement.

inheritance tax (in-HER-it-ence): A state tax assessed on an heir receiving an inheritance. This is different from an estate tax that is assessed to an entire estate.

After Frank's father died, Frank found out he had to pay an inheritance tax to the state.

in-house (in house): Work that is done within an organization as opposed to contracting it out.

We have an in-house advertising staff.

initial (in-ISH-el): The beginning.

The initial product from Widgets Inc. was the Model T widget.

Initial Public Offering (IPO) (in-ISH-el PUB-lik of-FER-ing): The first time stock is offered for sale to the public. This is the step that takes a company from a private company to a public company.

Stuff Company is scheduling an initial public offering for next month in order to raise capital for a major expansion.

initiative (in-IH-she-ah-tive): Taking an action without waiting to be told what to do.

George showed initiative by putting together a mailing list of potential clients.

injunction (in-JUNK-shun): A preventive legal action used to stop a specific activity.

Widgets Inc. was granted an injunction against its competitor, Stuff Company, to prevent it from selling widgets with the Widgets Inc. logo.

in kind (in kinde): The same type.

> *Widgets Inc. and Stuff Company make in-kind widgets.*

in-kind distribution (in kind dis-trih-BU-shun): The dispersing of property rather than selling it and dispersing money.

> *Jonathan Widget left a 1,000-acre piece of land after his death and each of his four children inherited 250 acres. It was an in-kind distribution.*

inkjet printer (INK-jet PRINT-er): A type of printer that sprays tiny dots of ink on paper.

> *Sue is happy with her inkjet printer because it is quiet and has a higher resolution than her old dot matrix printer.*

inland carrier (IN-land KAR-re-er): A transportation company that takes goods from a dock and distributes them throughout the country.

> *The European company, Le Widget, relies on an inland carrier to bring its widgets from the docks of New York to markets across America.*

innovation (in-no-VA-shun): A new product or service.

> *Widgets Inc. has a new innovation for its high-tech widgets that many customers have already started using.*

input (IN-put): Data that is put into a computer to be processed.

> *I used my keyboard to give my computer input on sales figures from last month.*

input-output (IO) (IN-put OUT-put): How a computer operates. Information is put in and information comes out.

> *Let me know if you like this new software and its way of input-output.*

inquiry (in-KWIR-e): An examination of facts during a search for information.

The auditor is conducting an inquiry into whether the missing funds were embezzled or just lost somehow.

inside information (IN-SIDE in-for-MA-shun): Information that would only be known by those inside a company.

One of the officers of Widgets Inc. was trying to sell stock before the quarterly report became public. This was using inside information to make a trade, and the officer knew it was illegal to make such a trade.

insider (IN-side-er): A person inside the top level of a company who knows information about that company that is not generally known to the public.

When Alfred Noethics tried to sell his stock before the quarterly report was released, he was ripe for investigation because he is an insider.

insider trading (IN-side-er TRADE-ing): Trading in securities by someone who has inside information about a company. This kind of trading is illegal.

Alfred Noethics engaged in insider trading by trying to unload stock before the quarterly report was released.

insolvency (in-SOL-ven-se): The inability to pay bills.

Widgets Inc. has been racked by major financial problems and now the company is facing insolvency.

inspection (in-SPEK-shun): A physical examination of a piece of property, products, or documents.

Before the company received an occupancy permit for its new building, the building had to pass an inspection.

inspector general (in-SPEK-ter JEN-er-el): The federal office that audits and investigates federal agencies.

News agencies are always interested in any report by the inspector general to Congress.

installment (in-STALL-ment): A regular payment made to reduce a debt.

It is important when you have a mortgage not to miss an installment.

installment sale (in-STALL-ment sale): A sale that includes an agreement that the purchaser will pay for the product with a series of payments over a given period of time.

The new 35-inch television we bought was purchased as an installment sale.

installment settlement (in-STALL-ment SET-tl-ment): A death benefit payment from a life insurance policy that is made in installments.

Max Life's family was surprised to find out his insurance policy didn't pay a lump sum but was instead an installment settlement.

institutional advertising (in-stih-TU-shun-el ad-ver-TIZE-ing): Type of advertising that presents an image of a company rather than focusing on any particular product.

Widgets Inc. put out some institutional advertising to show it is a company that cares about the environment.

institutional lender (in-stih-TU-shun-el LEND-er): An entity, such as a savings and loan, which uses money from depositors or customers to invest in loans.

Widgets Inc. went to an institutional lender to apply for a loan to expand its factory.

institutional trader (in-stih-TU-shun-el TRADE-er): An entity that trades in a high volume of securities.

A mutual fund is an institutional trader, and so is a bank or a pension fund.

instrument (IN-struh-ment): A legal document that makes a record of some action.

The instrument that the company used to pay the consultant was a check.

insurability (in-SHURE-ah-BIL-ih-te): Meeting the set of standards set up by insurance companies to qualify for insurance.

The fact that Zachary is a smoker could hurt his insurability with some companies.

insurable interest (in-SHURE-ah-bl IN-ter-est): Something that can be protected by insurance.

The Widgets Inc. factory is an insurable interest.

insurance (in-SHURE-ens): A system of covering risk with a financial guarantee of payment for a loss by the insurance company and promise of a monthly premium payment by the insured.

Widgets Inc. has health insurance for its employees, fire insurance for its building, and liability insurance to protect it from lawsuits.

insurance agent (in-SHURE-ens A-jent): A person who represents an insurance company in the sales and service of an insurance policy.

Betty talked to her insurance agent when she bought her homeowner's policy and five years later when she filed a claim.

insurance broker (in-SHURE-ens BROKE-er): A person who works for the insured by helping them find a company offering the best package for the best price.

An insurance broker is independent and works with more than one company.

insurance rate (in-SHURE-ens rate): The amount it costs for insurance.

Insurance rates are going up this year.

insurgent (in-SUR-jent): A rebel, one who challenges the status quo and the present leadership.

There is infighting at Exhaustive Express Inc., where an insurgent group led by marketing president Fred Fighter is challenging the leadership of CEO Mortimer Doodle.

intangible property (in-TAN-jih-bl PROP-er-te): Documents that represent real value or property.

Stock certificates from Widgets Inc. are intangible property.

integrate (IN-teh-grate): To bring together different parts of a product or to bring together different departments.

The production of widgets at Widgets Inc. integrates the three stages of the process.

integrated circuit (IN-teh-grate-ed SIR-kit): A silicon chip made up of many electronic transistors and other elements.

The integrated circuit in a computer that runs all the mathematical and logical equations is called the microprocessor.

integrity (in-TEG-rih-te): An admirable trait that includes honesty, reliability, and a sense of right and wrong.

Al Perkins liked doing deals with Susan Brown because he knew she had absolute integrity.

intellectual property (in-tel-LEK-chu-el PROP-er-te): Any creation or idea that is worth real value.

> *The jokes written for Jay Leno and David Letterman are considered intellectual property.*

interest (IN-ter-est): The cost of borrowing money over a given time period, or the payment to a depositor for the use of their money over a time period.

> *Donna asked the salesman how much money she would be paying in interest on her car loan.*

interest income (IN-ter-est IN-kum): Money earned from an investment.

> *Gretchen's interest income from her bank account is quite low.*

interest rate (IN-ter-est rate): The percentage payback for the use of money over a given period of time.

> *The annual interest rate for a five-year CD is 7 percent.*

interest rate swap (IN-ter-est rate swap): An agreement to turn a fixed rate loan into a variable rate loan, or vice versa.

> *The Smiths purchased their home with a variable rate loan but when interest rates fell they did an interest rate swap and acquired a fixed-rate loan at the new low rate.*

interface (IN-ter-fase): A computer interaction between two different ways of handling data.

> *We have to try to get an interface between your word processing software and mine so that I can read the report that you wrote.*

interim audit (IN-ter-im audit): An audit of financial records that is conducted at a time other than the end of a year or the end of a quarter.

> *Widgets Inc. does a couple of interim audits a quarter.*

interindustry competition (in-ter-IN-dus-tre kom-peh-TISH-un): Competition between companies that are in different industries.

When Washington Elementary School decided to put in a new playground, there was some interindustry competition between makers of slides and makers of monkey bars.

intermediary (in-ter-ME-de-ah-re): Any individual that tries to set up a deal between two parties.

The real estate broker is an intermediary between the house seller and buyer.

intermediate term (in-ter-ME-de-et term): A length of time that falls between short term and long term. The precise time span depends on the context.

An intermediate term for a bond is between three and ten years.

intermediation (in-ter-mede-A-shun): Giving money to an intermediary to invest.

You have to contact a broker for intermediation into the stock market.

intermittent production (in-ter-MIT-ent pro-DUK-shun): A method of running a production line in which several different products are produced on it at different times.

Widgets Inc. is running its production line on intermittent production between its high-tech widget, low-tech widget, and its other product, the doohickey.

internal audit (in-TER-nel AW-dit): An examination of financial records by an accountant employed by the company.

Midway though every quarter, Widgets Inc. conducts an internal audit of all of its departments.

internal check (in-TER-nel chek): Security measures taken by a company to protect itself from theft.

Widgets Inc. kept two attack dogs on the premises as an internal check.

Internal Revenue Service (IRS) (in-TER-nel REV-eh-nu SER-vis): The federal agency that collects taxes.

Every April 15, millions are writing checks to the IRS.

international cartel (in-ter-NASH-un-el kar-TEL): A group that operates on a worldwide basis.

The group OPEC, which stands for Organization of Petroleum Exporting Countries, is an international cartel.

International Monetary Fund (IMF) (in-ter-NASH-un-el MON-eh-tar-e fund): An international organization, headquartered in Washington D.C., that lends money to developing nations with the goal of stabilizing currencies and lowering trade barriers.

The International Monetary Fund played a large role in the stabilization of the wooden shebango coin of the tropical island nation of Paradise.

international union (in-ter-NASH-un-el YUNE-yun): A union that has local affiliations in many different countries.

The International Longshoremen's and Warehousemen's Union is an international union.

Internet (In-TER-net): The interconnection of computer networks to one another.

You can spend all day looking around the Internet and never get bored.

Internet relay chat (IRC) (In-TER-net RE-lay chat): A method of holding conversations on the Internet in which a group of people type in entries and converse in a forum.

I have met many friends through Internet relay chat.

interpreter (in-TER-pret-er): A person who translates foreign languages so that two people who do not speak the same language can have a conversation.

The president of Widgets Inc. went to Russia and brought along an interpreter so he could communicate with potential Russian customers.

interstate commerce (IN-ter-state KOM-mers): Business activity that is conducted across state lines.

Widgets Inc. ships its widgets to every state in the country; therefore, it is involved in interstate commerce.

interview (IN-ter-vu): A conversation between two people for the purpose of discovering whether the applicant is the right person to be hired for a job.

Adam was nervous before his job interview.

intestate (in-TES-tate): A person who dies without leaving a will.

Sue's father died intestate, but she inherited his property anyway because no one contested her inheritance.

inure (in-URE): To come into use.

Frank's parents gave him a gift of land that inures to him on his twenty-fifth birthday.

inventory (IN-ven-toh-re): The value of a company's goods. This includes everything from raw materials to finished goods.

The most widely used methods of inventory evaluation are first in, first out (FIFO) and last in, first out (LIFO).

inventory control (IN-ven-toh-re kun-TROLE): A system of keeping track of inventory to ensure stock is maintained and to prevent theft.

The manager at the convenience store warned his new employee not to even think of stealing a candy bar because the store has very tight inventory control.

inventory planning (IN-ven-toh-re PLAN-ing): A strategy for keeping enough inventory to meet needs but not too much to add to costs.

Inventory planning is one of the most important parts of Zelda's job at Widgets Inc.

inventory turnover (IN-ven-toh-re TURN-O-ver): The number of times inventory is sold and replaced during a given accounting period.

Keep an eye on inventory turnover because that will give us an idea if we are doing a good job of inventory planning.

inverted yield curve (in-VERT-ed yeeld kurv): Circumstance in which short-term interest rates are higher than long-term interest rates.

There is currently an inverted yield curve on interest rates, but that is uncommon.

investment (in-VEST-ment): The purchase of property or a security with the expectation that it will grow in value.

Alan bought stock in Widgets Inc. with plans to hold it as an investment until his daughter is old enough for college.

investment advisor (in-VEST-ment ad-VIZE-er): A person who is paid to give financial advice on what are the best investments for a person, depending on the person's particular circumstances.

Before I invested in the stock market, I set up a meeting with a financial advisor who strongly recommended I buy stock in Widgets Inc.

investment club (in-VEST-ment klub): A club in which a group of people pool their money together and make investments as a group.

Stan found it was more interesting and fun to be in an investment club than to make investments on his own.

investment company (in-VEST-ment KUM-pah-ne): A regulated company that makes investments for others.

Sam took his money to an investment company because he wanted to rely on the expertise of professionals.

investment income (in-VEST-ment IN-kum): Money earned from investments, including dividends, interest, and profits from the sale of investments.

The stock market has risen this year and so has my investment income.

investor relations department (in-VEST-er re-LAY-shuns de-PART-ment): A deparment in a large public firm that is responsible for ensuring that proper information is released to investors and for dealing with requests of investors.

Mary contacted the investor relations department at Widgets Inc. to get information about the company's performance in past years.

involuntary unemployment (in-VOL-un-tar-e un-em-PLOY-ment): The inability to get a job in one's chosen field.

After John was laid off from Widgets Inc., he tried desperately to find another firm that would hire him as a widget engineer, but he couldn't find such a job. John was in the midst of involuntary unemployment.

iota (i-O-tah): A very small amount.

The union official complained that the president of Widgets Inc. does not have an iota of concern about any workers at his factory.

irrevocable (ir-REVE-o-kah-bl): Something that cannot be changed.

Stan was told that if he agreed to terms, the job offer was irrevocable.

issue (ISH-u): Securities sold by a company at a specific time.

The stock from Widgets Inc. is a new issue.

itemized deduction (I-tem-ized de-DUK-chun): Specific, point-by-point deductions.

The accountant told the freelance consultant to put together a list of itemized deductions from business expenses.

itinerant worker (i-TIN-er-ent WORK-er): A worker who works for different people and continually changes jobs.

Sam, the widget consultant, is an itinerant worker.

Japanese-style teamwork (jap-ah-NESE stile TEME-wurk): Method of getting employees to work together by convincing them to think like a team and motivating them to want to be productive.

Widgets Inc. has changed its mode of operation from a domineering management style to Japanese-style teamwork, and the company has found it successful.

jawboning (JAW-bone-ing): Using the authority of a high office to influence others.

The president of Widgets Inc. was jawboning a local reporter to try and get some good press for the company.

jobber (JOB-ber): A middleman between manufacturers and retailers.

Widgets Inc. sold to regional jobbers who then sold the widgets to retail outlets in their area.

job classification (job CLASS-ih-fih-KA-shun): A way of putting jobs into categories in order to compare work and compensation.

When Steve was promoted from widget maker to foreman, his job classification was changed and his pay went up.

job evaluation (job e-val-u-A-shun): The method of determining how much a job is worth to an organization.

The management of Widgets Inc. is doing job evaluations for every position on its factory floor.

job lot (job lot): The size of a production run that is ordered by one job order.

The job lot from our latest job order is 20,000 widgets.

job order (job OR-der): An order given by management to start a specific production run.

We just received a job order for 20,000 widgets.

job placement (job PLACE-ment): Assignment of a person to a job that he is qualified for and that management needs filled.

Andy from personnel is in charge of job placement for the production line of the new high-tech widgets.

job security (job seh-KYU-rih-te): Freedom from worry that a job is about to be eliminated.

Evan liked the fact that Widgets Inc. has grown every year for fifty years. It gave him a sense of job security.

job shop (job shop): A business that takes orders rather than manufacturing products it must try to sell.

Alice went to a job shop to get a special part made quickly for the company's broken widget press.

job specification (job SPES-ih-fih-KA-shun): A description of the requirements of a job including experience and education.

Sue was going to apply for the manager's job in her department until she read the job specification and realized the company is looking for someone with a master's degree.

joint product cost (joint pro-DUKT kost): An accounting method that assesses the costs of more than one product that arise from a single manufacturing process.

When Widgets Inc. figured the joint product costs of widgets and doohickeys, which come off the production line together, it based the costs on the relative selling price of each.

joint venture (joint VEN-chure): An agreement between two people or companies to work on a project together.

The Harris Condominium project is a joint venture between Harris Company and Stratford Inc.

journal (JOUR-nel): An accounting book that records transactions.

I want to see the journal updates about transactions last month.

journal entry (JOUR-nel EN-tre): An entry in an accounting journal that includes equal debit and credit numbers.

The accountant made a journal entry about the purchase of 1,000 widgets.

journeyman (JOUR-ne-men): Someone who has mastered a craft and finished an apprenticeship.

After five years as an apprentice, Stephanie is finally a journeyman widget maker.

joystick (joy stik): A device with a handle that is used to play a computer game.

Matthew told his son to give him the joystick and he'd show him how to play the game.

judgment (JUDJ-ment): A ruling of a court to pay money.

The consumer group won a judgment against Widgets Inc. to pay $5 million because of the dangerous widgets it knowingly put on the market.

jumbo certificate of deposit (JUM-bo ser-TIF-ih-ket of de-POZ-it): A CD that has a minimum deposit of $100,000.

When Bill's son made it to the NBA and received a $14 million signing bonus, he put much of his money into jumbo certificates of deposit.

junior mortgage (JUNE-yur MOR-gej): A mortgage that does not hold a claim against a property until the main mortgage is paid.

After Stuff Company went bankrupt, the holder of the junior mortgage on the property knew that he would probably not get paid by the auction of the property.

junk bond (junk bond): Bonds with a low rating. These are risky bonds.

My financial advisor recommended I keep my money out of junk bonds.

junk fax (junk fax): A fax message that was not requested and was sent by a mass marketer.

Every day our fax machine is tied up by junk fax.

junk mail (junk male): Mail that is sent out by a mass marketer in an attempt to sell some item.

Every day my mailbox is clogged with junk mail.

jurisdiction (ju-ris-DIK-shun): The legal power and authority to hear and decide cases.

Before you file suit, you need to know which court has jurisdiction.

jurisprudence (ju-ris-PRU-dens): The science of law.

I have the best lawyer in the world. He is an expert in jurisprudence.

just compensation (just kom-pen-SA-shun): Fair payment for a piece of property taken by eminent domain.

When the state built a highway and took Sam's land by eminent domain, he received just compensation.

just-in-time (JIT) (just in time): A strategy of either manufacturing or acquiring inventory when it is needed rather than stocking extra amounts.

In order to reduce inventory costs, Widgets Inc. has gone with a just-in-time approach.

kangaroo bonds (kan-gah-ROO bonds): Bonds in Australian currency.

Widgets Inc. issued kangaroo bonds to finance its new plant in Sydney, Australia.

Keogh plan (KE-o plan): Retirement plan for the self-employed.

One of the first things Linda did after starting her consulting business was to set up a Keogh plan.

Keynesian economics (KEENZ-e-en e-ko-NOM-iks): Economic theory devised by former British economist John Maynard Keynes, who believed government intervention could keep the economy steady by adjusting levels of spending and taxation.

Some economists believe in Keynesian economics, while others think it is meddling in the operation of a free market.

keypunch (ke punch): Data entry method that involves punching holes in a computer card that can be read by a computer.

Sue's first job was as a keypunch operator.

kickback (KIK-bak): An illegal payoff to someone who has great influence in how a contract is awarded.

The president of Widgets Inc. was indicted for making a kickback to the mayor just before the city awarded a contract to buy widgets from Widgets Inc.

killing (KIL-ing): A big profit.

Amy made a killing in the stock market.

kiosk (ke-OSK): A stand that holds a specific type of merchandise from one company and is in a visible part of a retail store.

Widgets Inc. tried to get a widgets kiosk placed near every register of Wal-Mart.

kiting (KITE-ing): Going to two or more banks and depositing and drawing checks between accounts.

When money was low, Elsie found herself kiting in order to stay above water while she waited for her freelance check to come in.

knee-jerk (nee jerk): A quick involuntary action or decision made without thought.

The president of Widgets Inc. fired the entire marketing department because the last marketing campaign was unsuccessful, causing many in the department to cite past successes and to say the firing was a knee-jerk reaction.

know-how (no how): Knowledge to be able to do something.

Sandy has the know-how to write specialized software for our company.

knowledge intensive (NOL-ej in-TEN-siv): A role in a business that requires a lot of training, education, and specific knowledge.

> *The new position we are creating for a widget software engineer is very knowledge intensive.*

know-your-customer rule (no yur KUS-tum-er rule): An ethical rule for brokerage houses that are making recommendations to customers. The rule states that the brokerage must know certain financial information about the customer to ensure it is not recommending too risky a course of action.

> *If you follow the know-your-customer rule, you will not make recommendations that could bankrupt someone.*

kudos (KU-doze): Credit given for an achievement.

> *Mary received kudos from the company for her excellent sales record this month.*

labor intensive (LA-bur in-TEN-siv): Business activity that requires a larger payout for labor than for capital.

> *Computer programming is labor intensive.*

ladder portfolio (LAD-der port-FO-le-o): A way of staggering the maturity of bonds that one invests in, in order to be ready to take advantage of the fluctuation of interest rates.

> *Stuart has a ladder portfolio so that if interest rates are low he can reinvest money in short-term bonds, and if they are high he can invest in longer-term bonds.*

Laffer Curve (LAF-fer kurv): Statistical curve, named after U.S. economist Arthur Laffer, that states that for a while an increase in a tax rate will increase tax revenues, but at some point the rate will get so high as to actually make revenues start to drop.

> *Many people who are upset with taxes point to the Laffer Curve as evidence that a high tax rate will even hurt tax revenues.*

laggard industry (LAG-gerd IN-dus-tre): An industry that does not keep up with a national economy in terms of key indicators such as employment and output.

It appears that the apparel industry is a laggard industry in this country, yet it is thriving on cheap labor overseas.

lagging indicators (LAG-ing IN-dih-ka-turs): A number of indicators that follow behind changes in the overall economy.

The economy started picking up a year ago, but employment, a lagging indicator, just recently started growing.

laissez-faire (LES-a-FAIR): A theory of economics that holds that a free market without government interference is the best way to grow an economy.

The president of Widgets Inc. fought vigorously against new regulations for his industry by claiming that a laissez-faire approach would be the best strategy.

laptop computer (LAP-top kum-PUTE-er): A small computer that can fit on your lap and be carried from place to place.

This laptop computer is the best investment I ever made because I can work on my cross-country plane flights.

last in, first out (LIFO) (last in first out): A method of accounting for inventory in which the last items brought in are considered the first items sold. This method shows lower income while inventory prices rise.

In order to show lower income, Widgets Inc. uses the LIFO method of inventory.

late trading (late TRADE-ing): Trading that occurs late in the business day.

The stock market plunged for a good part of the day but rallied almost all the way back in late trading.

law of large numbers (law of larj NUM-bers): Mathematical premise used in figuring insurance rates that states if a group of policyholders is large enough, the company can accurately predict how many will suffer a loss.

> *The reason why sixteen-year-old males have the highest auto insurance rates is simply a matter of the law of large numbers. Although not every sixteen-year-old male is a risky driver, the number that are is proportionately larger than any other demographic group.*

leading indicators (LEDE-ing IN-dih-ka-turs): The indicators that predict future economic activity in the U.S.

> *The president pointed to good news from all leading indicators as evidence that he is doing a good job getting the economy going.*

lead time (lede time): The amount of time between when an order is placed and when it is received.

> *We need to know what the lead time is on that order of widgets because if it's too long, we should cancel the order and try to get them from another company.*

learning curve (LURN-ing kurv): A description of how long it takes an employee to become more efficient.

> *Sue's last job with the company had a short learning curve and she was up to speed within a week, but her new job has a steep learning curve and she has still not gotten fully acclimated, even though she has been on the job for a month.*

lease (lese): A contract that deals with rent.

> *Stuart signed a three-year lease for a Mercedes.*

ledger (LEDJ-er): A book of accounts of a company.

> *The president of Widgets Inc. kept a close eye on the ledger to see which accounts were up to date and which were overdue.*

legal liability (LE-gel li-ah-BIL-IH-TE): An obligation to pay a certain amount of money within a specified time as an exchange for a current benefit.

We have a legal liability to pay our attorney within thirty days.

legal tender (LE-gel TEN-der): Paper money and coins as well as Federal Reserve notes.

Matthew was having credit problems and found that many places wouldn't accept his checks. They all wanted legal tender.

lender (LEN-der): Individual or company that lends money with the expectation of being repaid the full amount plus interest.

When Arnold wanted to start a business, he went to a local lender to apply for a business loan.

letter of recommendation (LET-ter of re-kuh-men-DAY-shun): A letter from an auditor to a client, evaluating the company's current accounting system and making recommendations on how to improve it.

Widgets Inc. has received a letter of recommendation stating that it should do a better job of keeping records in accounts receivable.

letter-quality (LET-ter KWAL-ih-te): A description of the ability of an electronic printer to be able to mimic the quality of a typewriter.

My new printer is excellent. It puts out letter-quality documents very fast.

leverage (LEV-er-ej): Using borrowed money to increase the ability of a company to buy things.

Widgets Inc. has leverage to buy a new widget press, with the expectation that the new press will increase profits.

leveraged buyout (LBO) (LEV-er-ejd BY-out): Using borrowed money to buy a company.

> *Stuff Company is attempting a leveraged buyout of the much larger Widgets Inc.*

life cycle (life SI-kl): The progression of a product through stages, from development to decline.

> *Experts estimate the life cycle of the new high-tech widget will be less than five years. By then, there will probably be an even more advanced product on the market.*

limited partner (LIM-it-ed PART-ner): A partner in a company who does not have any management responsibility and who has no liability beyond the capital invested.

> *Mary has used her large inheritance to invest in Widgets Inc. She is a limited partner and does not spend any time managing the company.*

liquid (LIH-kwid): Having an adequate amount of cash to cover short-term liabilities.

> *Widgets Inc. is a very liquid company with plenty of available cash.*

liquid asset (LIH-kwid ASS-set): Something of value that is either cash or easily convertible to cash.

> *Treasury bills are liquid assets.*

liquidation (lih-kwid-A-shun: Closing down a business and selling everything to pay off debts and to give any remaining cash to the owners.

> *Stuff Company failed to compete in the widget market and is undergoing liquidation.*

liquidation price (lih-kwid-A-shun prise): The price a company receives when it is liquidating its assets. The price is below market value.

Stuff Company went bankrupt and sold all of its assets at a liquidation price that was very low.

liquidity (lih-KWID-ih-te): The ability to convert an asset quickly into cash without losing value.

Stocks have a high liquidity, but real estate, which takes longer to sell for a fair value, does not.

load fund (lode fund): A mutual fund that has a sales charge from a brokerage firm.

Mary invested in a load fund that she felt was a strong fund and worth paying the sales charge.

loan commitment (lone kum-MIT-ment): A formal agreement to lend a specific amount of money that must be repaid at a certain interest rate in a specified time.

Jane is happy because she received the loan commitment for her new business today.

local area network (LAN) (LO-kel A-re-ah NET-wurk): A network of individual computers that are connected by cable.

Dave's high school has all of its computers on a local area network.

lock-in rate (lok in rate): Offer from a lender to guarantee an interest rate for a loan.

The bank has committed to a lock-in rate of 7 percent for our loan.

log (log): A record of how an item is used. The record is for internal company purposes.

If you check the log for that database you will see who was in it and when they used it.

logo (LO-go): A symbol that represents a company.

The Nike swoosh is one of the most recognized logos in the world.

loss (loss): When expenses are higher than revenues.

Widgets Inc. experienced a loss on its high-tech widgets that were expensive to develop but never sold very well.

loss carryback (loss KAR-re bak): Balancing the net loss for a current year against the net revenues for the previous three years. This accounting strategy allows a company to receive a refund for the taxes paid in those previous three years.

Stuff Company used loss carryback to account for its loss this year.

loss carry forward (loss KAR-re FOR-werd): Balancing the net loss for a current year against expected net revenues for future years.

Stuff Company used loss carry forward to account for its loss this year.

loss leader (loss LEDE-er): Something that is sold in a retail store at a loss. The idea is to use that item to draw people to the store in the hope that they will purchase other items.

The department store advertised widgets at a price below cost in the hope that the loss leader would bring people in the store to shop for many items.

loss of utility (loss of u-TIL-ih-te): An accounting term meaning loss of usefulness that brings about a loss in value.

Widgets Inc. is writing down its new widget press for loss of utility because the machine is already obsolete in today's rapidly changing market.

lump-sum distribution (lump sum dis-trih-BU-shun): A payment of a retirement benefit all at one time.

Larry received a lump-sum distribution of his retirement benefit, which he liked better than the idea of getting it in installments.

lump-sum purchase (lump sum PUR-ches): Buying two or more items from a single seller and paying for both in one payment.

The Smiths made a lump-sum purchase of their house and the land.

machine hour (mah-SHEEN our): A method of allocating costs for overhead for work in process.

We like to keep an eye on machine-hour costs to see what the cost of overhead is for our work in process.

machine language (mah-SHEEN LANG-gwej): Direct instructions to a computer written in binary code.

Steve has a problem using machine language because it is hard to understand without the use of words.

machine loading (mah-SHEEN LODE-ing): The ability of a consumer machine to automatically set itself up without human assistance.

Sara bought a machine-loading camera. It automatically loads the film.

machine scanning (mah-SKAN-ing): Optical tool used to read printed matter into a computer.

Grocery stores use machine scanning to read in bar codes.

Macintosh (MACK-in-tosh): The easy-to-use computer by Apple that has a graphical interface.

My son's first-grade class has a Macintosh.

macros (MAK-ro): A single computer command that combines several commands into one keystroke.

When I get new software, I like to set up my macros right away so I can save time.

macroeconomics (MAK-ro-ek-o-NOM-iks): The study of a nation's overall economy with an eye on big-picture items such as inflation, unemployment, and prices.

The new trade agreement and unemployment rates are interesting to those who study macroeconomics but not to me. I run a hamburger joint. I'm worried about the price of ketchup.

Madison Avenue (MAD-ih-sun AV-eh-nu): The home of many of the world's largest advertising agencies. Madison Avenue has become a general term meaning the professionals who try to sell us things.

Some people say you can blame Madison Avenue because of the pervasiveness of sex in our popular culture.

mail fraud (male fraud): A direct-mail inducement to buy something that uses fraudulent claims as part of its spiel.

Widgets Inc. sent out a flyer claiming its widgets can be used to upgrade the power of your computer, when really all they can do is rest on your box as a decoration. The company has been charged with mail fraud for that promotion.

mailing list (MAIL-ing list): A prepared list of potential customers to be targeted by direct mail.

Ever since I donated money to Save the Chipmunks, I have been on mailing lists of many environmental groups.

mainframe computer (MANE-frame kum-PUTE-er): A large computer that has the power for many users to hook into with a keyboard and monitor.

Widgets Inc. had an old mainframe computer that served the company well, but last year the company bought PCs for everyone.

maintenance (MANE-teh-nens): Taking care of equipment and fixing what is broken.

Widgets Inc. has a strict maintenance program on its factory equipment in the hope that problems can be avoided by regularly checking each machine.

majority shareholder (mah-JOR-ih-te SHARE-HOLD-er): A shareholder who controls more than half the shares of a corporation.

Edgar Widget is the majority shareholder in Widgets Inc.

major medical insurance (MA-jur MED-ik-el in-SHURE-ens): A supplemental type of health insurance that will pay for major medical disasters not covered by regular health insurance.

After the car accident, Stan's family was happy that he had major medical insurance, since he was hospitalized for months.

make-or-buy decision (make or bi de-SIZH-un): Decision whether to make a component needed for the core manufacturing process or to buy it.

Widgets Inc. is facing a make-or-buy decision on whether to manufacture its own doohickeys or buy them from Stuff Company.

managed care (MAN-ejd care): Health care delivery system in which a company has an agreement with a group of doctors. The doctors provide care at a discount, and the company promises to bring all of its employee's health problems exclusively to the doctors.

Widgets Inc. offers a managed care health plan to its employees, but Sue didn't like it because her doctor is not in the plan.

management (MAN-ej-ment): The decision makers in a company.

Employees are waiting to hear from management about their concerns for safety in the factory.

management by crisis (MAN-ej-ment bi KRI-sis): A shortsighted way of running a company by constantly reacting to problems rather than doing any long-range planning.

> *Stuart complained that his company has no vision. "It's just management by crisis," he said. "We never know what big decisions will be made next."*

management by objectives (MBO) (MAN-ej-ment bi ob-JEK-TIVS): A way of running a company that tries to get management and employees to agree on common performance goals.

> *Sara liked her new job because the company is run by management by objectives. "I know what is expected of me and what will happen if I reach my goals and what will happen if I don't."*

management by walking around (MBWA) (MAN-ej-ment bi WAK-ing ah-ROUND): A way of running a company that emphasizes the importance of making interpersonal contact with employees.

> *In a speech, the president of the company said, "I believe in management by walking around, so I am sure to get down to the factory floor at least once a week to see how things are going."*

Management Information Systems (MIS) (MAN-ej-ment in-for-MA-shun SIS-tems): The way that information is organized and distributed, especially with regard to databases.

> *The MIS department has put in a request for a new computer system.*

mandate (MAN-date): An authoritative order.

> *I received a mandate from management to hire three new salespeople by the end of the month.*

manifest (MAN-ih-fest): A detailed account of everything that is being transported on a ship or in a vehicle. The manifest is put in a place that will be safe even in the event of an accident.

> *When the ship that sunk in the North Atlantic was found, investigators learned what cargo it carried by looking at the manifest.*

manipulation (mah-nip-u-LA-shun): Creating a false impression that the market is active by buying or selling securities.

> *Even though Edgar Widget knows manipulation is illegal, last week he tried to get the price of Widgets Inc. stock to drop by selling many of his shares at a low price. He hoped to see some Widgets stock drop in price and investors unload it so he could buy it all back at a discount.*

manual (MAN-u-el): A guidebook on how to use something or how to put something together.

> *The new high-tech widget is so complex that it comes with its own manual.*

manual skill (MAN-u-el skill): The ability to use one's hands in a dexterous way.

> *A brain surgeon has manual skill, and so does an architect.*

manufacturing (man-u-FAK-chure-ing): The process of making things.

> *"We are manufacturing widgets. Thousands and thousands of widgets. It requires many machines and many people," said the president of Widgets Inc.*

marginal cost (MAR-jin-el kost): The change in cost that occurs when producing one or less than one unit of an item.

> *Wendy's job was to study the marginal cost of all the different types of widgets produced by her company to see which ones should have a bigger run.*

marginal property (MAR-jin-el PROP-er-te): Property that does not make a large profit.

The mortgage on the shopping plaza is $30,000, and the real estate company is bringing in $30,500 in rent. This is a marginal property.

marginal utility (MAR-jin-el u-TIL-ih-te): Additional fulfillment or usefulness gained by using one or more units of a product.

The marginal utility for chocolate bars is fairly high compared to the marginal utility for lawnmowers.

margin of profit (MAR-jin of PROF-it): The ratio of gross profits divided by net sales.

Management likes to keep an eye on the margin of profit.

markdown (MARK-down): Dropping the price of a retail item below its original price.

Jeffrey liked to shop at the factory outlet mall and look for mark-downs.

market (MAR-ket): The demand for a product, or the place where a product is sold.

There is a good market for widgets. Or . . . We are going to be taking our new high-tech widget onto the market.

marketability (MAR-ket-ah-BIL-ih-te): How easy it is to sell an item.

"Everybody needs a widget," declared the president of Widgets Inc. "The marketability of our products is very high."

market analysis (MAR-ket ah-NAL-ih-sis): A study of the potential of a company to expand within a market.

Stuff Company did a market analysis that showed the company could gain market share from Widgets Inc. if it could make a better, cheaper widget.

market area (MAR-ket A-re-ah): The geographic area from where most of the demand for a product originates.

> *The market area for the Widgets Inc. high-tech widget is, for some reason, the old Confederate states.*

market economy (MAR-ket e-KON-o-me): An economy that allows a free market to flourish and to determine the flow of goods and services.

> *Ever since the fall of the Berlin Wall, much of Eastern Europe has converted to a market economy.*

marketing (MAR-ket-ing): Promoting sales.

> *The rock star named Gimme Cash is an expert at marketing himself.*

market share (MAR-ket shar): The percentage of overall industry sales that belongs to one particular company or product.

> *Widgets Inc.'s new high-tech widget has captured a 50 percent market share of all widgets sold in the U.S.*

market value (MAR-ket VAL-u): An estimate of the price a property would sell for on the open market.

> *Our house was appraised at having a market value of $200,000.*

markup (MARK-up): The percentage that a wholesale price is raised to get it to the retail price.

> *The little country store had a 20 percent markup on the price of widgets.*

Maslow's Hierarchy of Needs (MAZ-loze HI-er-ark-ee of needs): Theory of motivational needs as developed by Abraham Maslow. The theory is that humans have five levels of needs. Once one level is satisfied, a person goes on to the next level. The five levels are physiological, safety, social, esteem, and self-actualization.

As a successful artist, George has fulfilled all of Maslow's Hierarchy of Needs.

mass appeal (mass ap-PEEAL): Nonspecific sales approach that is aimed at all possible consumers of a product.

Soft drink companies often use mass appeal to sell their soda.

mass communication (mass kum-mu-nih-KA-shun): Widely used media channels such as newspapers, magazines, radio and television stations.

Widgets Inc. launched a mass communication campaign to announce the new high-tech widget.

mass media (mass ME-de-ah): Wide array of media sources that are readily available, including television and radio stations, newspapers, magazines, advertisements, and billboards.

If you can get the word out about your product in the mass media, you have a great chance at success.

mass production (mass pro-DUK-shun): Manufacturing large quantities of a product using automated machinery and/or repetitive employee actions.

Staring at his huge factory floor, the president of Widgets Inc. said, "This is what I call mass production."

master lease (MAS-ter lese): A lease that holds priority over a sublease.

The master lease on the shopping center is for five years. You cannot have a sublease on one of the stores for six years.

Master of Business Administration (MBA) (MAS-ter of BIZ-ness ad-min-is-TRA-shun): A graduate degree in business. An MBA is in a specialty such as finance, management, or accounting.

Michelle worked for two years on Wall Street and then she went back to school to get her MBA. Now, she has a great job.

master plan (MAS-ter plan): A report about how to develop land. A master plan can be developed by a government planning agency or it can be put together privately by a group trying to develop a tract of real estate.

The town unveiled its master plan two weeks ago. The one part I didn't like was its call for zoning changes in my neighborhood.

master policy (MAS-ter POL-ih-se): An insurance policy that is issued to an employer for all of its employees.

So I turned to my friend and I said, "You work at the same place as I do. You have the exact same insurance as I do. Widgets Inc. has a master policy."

masthead (MAST-hed): Newspaper and magazine term meaning the actual name of the publication as printed at the top of the first page. Or . . . The box within the publication that lists the key editorial staff, the address, and phone number of the publication.

I like the graphics of the masthead of Widgetworld *magazine. Or . . . If you want to write a letter to the editor, check the masthead for the address.*

material (mah-TE-re-el): The stuff used in manufacturing.

The foreman said we do not have enough material to run all day.

materials handling (mah-TE-re-els HAN-dling): Moving and storing all forms of materials.

If you are in materials handling, you are charged with moving and storing supplies, products, scrap, everything.

materials management (mah-TE-re-els MAN-ej-ment): Managing anything that has to do with moving and storing materials.

Materials management is in charge of the warehouse and the transportation department.

mathematical model (math-eh-MAT-ik-el MOD-el): A mathematical representation of some real or hypothetical situation.

We are putting together a mathematical model of how different levels of inflation will affect our business.

matrix (MA-trix): A mathematical term for a table that has rows and columns full of some sort of analytical data.

If you do a matrix on that data, I bet you will see a pattern.

matrix organization (MA-trix OR-gen-i-ZA-shun): Organization in which project specialists such as engineers and scientists are dedicated both to their project and to their department.

Widgets Inc. is trying to become a matrix organization, but not all of the independent-minded scientists are buying into it.

mature market (mah-CHURE MAR-ket): A market in which the demand for a product has stabilized.

The automobile market is a mature market, while the computer market is not.

maturity (mah-CHU-rih-te): The date when a legal right kicks in.

The bond is redeemable at its full price upon maturity.

maturity value (mah-CHU-rih-te VAL-u): The amount of money given to the owner of a life insurance policy who lives to a certain age.

The maturity value on my life insurance policy is $50,000 if I make it to eighty.

maximum foreseeable loss (MFL) (MAX-ih-mum for-SE-uh-bl loss): Insurance term for the most expensive loss possible if a catastrophe such as a fire or tornado occurred.

> *After a tornado ripped through the small town where Jim is an insurance agent, he began looking up the maximum foreseeable loss numbers because he knew he would be hearing from many of his clients.*

maximum practical capacity (MAX-ih-mum PRAK-tih-kel ka-PASS-ih-te): The busiest a factory can be while still being efficient. Also called practical capacity.

> *Considering the number of sick days we average around here, and that at any given time between 5 and 15 percent of our staff is on vacation, I'd say we are running at our maximum practical capacity.*

maximum probable loss (MPL) (MAX-ih-mum PROB-ah-bl loss): A guess as to what a loss will cost if every safety factor works as it is supposed to work.

> *The maximum probable loss if there is a fire in here is fairly low because we have a state-of-the-art sprinkler system.*

media (ME-de-ah): The various avenues and/or purveyors of communication, including television, radio, newspapers, magazines, advertising, music, movies, and billboards.

> *Everyone complains about the power of the media, including the media.*

media buyer (ME-de-ah BI-er): A person in a company or in an advertising agency who is responsible for buying on-air advertising time as well as advertising space in printed media.

> *Jeffrey is a great media buyer. He knows where to buy advertisements, when to buy, and who to target.*

media plan (ME-de-ah plan): An advertising plan, with a time frame and a budget, specifying what media will be used in a campaign.

The marketing department unveiled a media plan for the summer season to executives.

mediation (me-de-A-shun): The use of a third party to help two conflicting parties reach a negotiated settlement. Unlike in arbitration, the third party in mediation has no powers to force a settlement.

The union and Widgets Inc. agreed to try mediation to break the contract impasse.

Medicaid (MED-ih-KADE): Health insurance assistance administered jointly by the federal government and states. The assistance goes to people with low income and limited assets.

Congress is talking about slashing some funds for Medicaid.

Medicare (MED-ih-kar): Federal health insurance for people sixty-five and older and for people with permanent disabilities.

My grandmother depends on Medicare to pay for all of her medical treatments.

Medigap (MED-ih-GAP): Special type of supplemental health insurance designed to cover things that are not covered by Medicare.

My grandmother is smart because she took out a Medigap policy to help her out in case Medicare doesn't cover something she needs.

medium of exchange (ME-de-um of ex-CHANJE): Money. A medium of exchange in modern cultures means something that is recognized by all to represent the same value.

The medium of exchange in the U.S. is the dollar, while on the island nation of Paradise, the medium of exchange is the wooden shebango.

medium-term bond (ME-de-um term bond): A bond that reaches maturity between two and ten years.

Ann invested $5,000 in a medium-term bond.

meeting of the minds (MEET-ing of the mindes): When parties agree to a contract.

Now that you have agreed to work for us in principle, let's discuss specifics so we can quickly come to a meeting of the minds.

megabyte (MB) (MEG-ah-BITE): A term for memory capacity in a computer, a megabyte is equal to one million bytes of information.

The hard drive on my computer has 800 megabytes of memory.

megahertz (MEG-ah-HERTZ): A measurement of how fast a computer system works.

My new computer has a 150 megahertz Pentium processor.

member bank (MEM-ber bank): A bank that is in the Federal Reserve System.

Widgets Inc. has its accounts in a member bank.

memorandum (mem-o-RAN-dum): An informal note.

The boss sent out a memorandum every Monday with a rambling description of how much he wants everyone to work harder.

memory (MEM-o-re): Electronic area within a computer in which data is stored.

My hard drive has 800 megabytes of memory.

menial (ME-ne-el): Work that is trivial and demeaning.

After Beth was fired for stealing, the only kind of work she could find was menial labor.

mentor (MEN-tur): An experienced person who gives advice to someone less experienced.

When I first started working at Widgets Inc., I was hooked up with Fred who became my mentor and really helped me to get off the ground.

menu (MEN-u): A list of options that appears on a computer screen.

Here, let me call up the menu, and then all you have to do is pick an option.

mercantile agency (MER-ken-tile A-jen-se): An information company that provides credit ratings to businesses.

Before we sold widgets to Stuff Company on credit, we checked on their reputation with a mercantile agency.

merchandise (MER-chen-dise): Everything sold at a retail level.

The owner of the local general store always tells people he has better merchandise than the big department stores.

merchant bank (MER-chent bank): A bank that is a financial player engaging in investing, negotiating mergers, counseling, and other activities.

If you go into the city, you may be able to find a merchant bank that can help you launch your automobile company.

merge (merj): Combining two companies into one financial entity.

After months of negotiations, Widgets Inc. and Stuff Company have announced they will merge to create a new company called Widgets Stuff.

merger (MERJ-er): A reorganization in which one company acquires another.

The merger of Widgets Inc. and Stuff Company resulted in Widgets Inc. getting bigger and Stuff Company ceasing to exist.

merit increase (MER-it in-KRESE): Pay raise given because of good performance on the job.

I received a merit increase this year.

metered mail (ME-terd mail): Mail stamped by a postage meter instead of a stamp.

All of our direct marketing goes out in metered mail.

microcomputer (MI-kro-kum-PUTE-er): A computer that has a micro-processor and is designed to be used by one person.

My new PC, like all PCs, is a microcomputer.

microeconomics (MI-kro-ek-o-NOM-iks): The study of specific economic units such as companies, cities, or households.

Dan the economist is not as concerned with the big picture as he is with the state of Widgets Inc. Dan knows a lot about Widgets Inc. and about microeconomics.

microprocessor (MI-kro-PROS-es-ur): A single integrated chip that serves as the central processing unit for a microcomputer.

My computer is very fast because I bought the newest micro-processor on the market.

Microsoft (MI-kro-soft): The company that developed the most common operating systems, MS-DOS and Windows.

I wish I owned stock in Microsoft because the value just keeps going up.

midcareer plateau (MID-kah-REER pla-TO): A stage in a middle manager's career when the current job is not challenging but the chances for advancement appear slim.

Steve became bored at his job when it became apparent to him that he had reached a midcareer plateau.

middle management (MID-dl MAN-ej-ment): Managers who run a specific department who report to higher-level managers.

John led a happy, comfortable life as a middle manager before his company started downsizing.

midnight deadline (MID-nite DED-line): When something is due at midnight of a certain day.

On April 15, there is a midnight deadline for filing taxes.

migrant worker (MI-grent WURK-er): A worker who moves to wherever there is employment. Many migrant workers are farm workers who harvest fruits and vegetables by hand.

The migrant workers traveled continually south, as the harvest season always came first in the north.

military-industrial complex (MIL-ih-tar-e in-DUS-tre-el KOM-plex): Term coined by President Dwight Eisenhower in his farewell address. It is a reference to how powerfully and closely tied the military and the industrial components of society are.

The speaker with the megaphone on the college campus said, "I'm telling you, man, the military-industrial complex is out to get all of us."

milking (MILK-ing): Using a situation to one's full advantage.

When the company sends me to Hawaii for that conference, I'll be milking it for some time on the beach as well.

minicomputer (MIN-e-kum-PUT-er): A computer smaller than a mainframe but larger than a PC.

We still have one old minicomputer that a couple of people are still hooked into, but everyone else now has their own PC.

minimum lease payments (MIN-ih-mum lese PAY-ments): Regular rent payments due.

Our minimum lease payment for the storefront is $2,000 a month.

minimum lot area (MIN-ih-mum lot A-re-ah): A zoning condition that does not allow any building lots to be smaller than a specific size.

Because of concerns about groundwater in my town, the minimum lot area is one acre.

minimum wage (MIN-ih-mum waje): A federal law setting the lowest allowed wage for any job. Or . . . The lowest allowed wage permitted by a union contract.

My son turns sixteen this year and he is hoping Congress raises the minimum wage. Or . . . My son just got a job at that steel plant that is a union plant. The minimum wage there is $12 an hour.

minority business (MI-nor-ih-te BIZ-ness): A business owned by a member of an underprivileged minority. These businesses are eligible for a percentage of U.S. government contracts that are earmarked to go to minority businesses.

The contract for the new government building included the stipulation that at least 5 percent of all work subcontracted must be subcontracted to a minority business.

miscellaneous itemized deductions (mis-sel-LA-ne-us I-tem-ized de-DUK-shuns): Expense deductions that do not fit any specific category of deductions. Included among these are job expenses, union dues, uniform expenses, and unreimbursed travel expenses.

I have a lot of receipts keeping track of miscellaneous itemized deductions.

mitigation of damages (mit-ih-GA-shun of DAM-ej-ez): A request by a defendant to lower the amount of damages owed to a plaintiff. Such a request is backed by evidence showing the plaintiff does not deserve the amount previously awarded.

> *Widgets Inc. asked for a mitigation of damages after showing that, out of the millions of people who bought its widgets, only one was seriously injured.*

mix (mix): The way different sounds are combined in a recording, film, or videotape.

> *We brought in a sound professional from New York City to do the mix on our latest widgets commercials.*

mixed signals (mixd SIG-nels): Communication sent out by one person that contradicts previous communication from the same person.

> *First management told us to get more salesmen out in the field, and then when we did, they told us our travel budget was way too high. We were getting really mixed signals.*

mode (mode): The way things work.

> *I like this company. It's always in a pretty casual mode as long as you get the work done.*

modem (MO-dem): Electronic device that converts computer data into telephone signals, and vice versa. Modems allow computers to send information back and forth across telephone lines.

> *I have a new high-speed modem.*

modus operandi (MO) (MO-dus OP-er-and-i): Method of operating. It usually means the characteristics of an operation that are traceable to a person or company.

> *Widgets Inc.'s modus operandi was to introduce its widgets to a town by getting in all the major retail outlets on one day.*

mogul (mo-GUL): A powerful, wealthy, important person.

By the end of his life, Jonathan Widget was often referred to as the widget mogul, because his company, Widgets Inc., controlled more than half the widget market.

momentum (mo-MEN-tum): The tendency of a market experiencing growth to continue to feel growth that feeds off of itself.

The market has been so strong lately, analysts wonder what could possibly stop the momentum.

monetary policy (MON-eh-tar-e POL-ih-se): The strategy of a nation's central bank to attempt to control the economy by controlling the money supply.

Some economists blame the monetary policy for the slow growth of the economy.

money market (MUN-e MAR-ket): A fund that is very liquid and allows the investor quick access to money. Money market funds are usually short-term debt instruments.

I always keep a few thousand dollars in money market funds just in case anything comes up.

money supply (MUN-e sup-PLI): All the money in an economy.

The Federal Reserve tends to adjust the money supply as a reaction to inflation rates.

monitor (MON-ih-tur): The screen of a computer.

I have a new fourteen-inch monitor on my computer that has incredible graphics.

monopoly (mo-NOP-o-le): An absence of competition because of the control of a market by one company or a small group of noncompeting companies.

> *Some people think that Widgets Inc. has almost a monopoly of the widgets market. There is very little competition, and all widgets are made the Widgets Inc. way.*

moot point (moot point): A fact raised that is no longer relevant to a discussion.

> *The prosecutor fumed, "It is a moot point to bring up the fact that the defendant used to be a good baseball coach. The important fact is that he took a knife and cut the wrist muscles of his rival's best pitcher."*

moonlighting (MOON-lite-ing): The act of working a second job, usually a night job.

> *After finishing his day in the factory at Widgets Inc., Sam could be found moonlighting as a tuxedoed drummer in a lounge band called The Electrics.*

morale (mo-RAHL): The collective mental and emotional state of a group.

> *Widgets Inc. is always looking for ways to improve the workplace of its employees, and it shows because the morale at the company is very high.*

moral suasion (MOR-el SWAY-zhun): Persuasion using logic and influence instead of force.

> *Stinkitup Company denied ever using a bribe to get permission for their dump. "We used moral suasion," said the president of the company.*

mortgage (MOR-gej): A debt instrument for the purchase of real estate in which the borrower has full access to the property, but a lien is on it until the loan is repaid.

The Smiths qualified for a mortgage to buy their first house.

mortgage interest deduction (MOR-gej IN-ter-est de-DUK-shun): Federal tax deduction allowed for interest paid on a mortgage of a first or second home.

One of the advantages in investing in a second home is the mortgage interest deduction.

motherboard (MUTH-er bord): The main board of a computer. The place that all other parts hook into to work together.

I soon discovered that my new computer came with a faulty motherboard.

motivation (mo-tiv-A-shun): An inner passion to get things done.

Arnold is not a very organized employee, but he has plenty of motivation. You never have to tell him twice to do something.

mouse (mous): A computer tool for inputting information. It is a handheld device that, when it moves, directs the movement of an arrow on the screen.

Just move your mouse and click on the icons and you will soon be surfing the Net.

mover and shaker (MOOV-er and SHAKE-er): An individual who can make things happen.

My uncle Bert is a real mover and shaker down at City Hall.

MS-DOS (em ess dos): A common computer operating system put out by Microsoft.

I don't have Windows, I have MS-DOS.

multinational companies (MUL-ti-NAH-shun-el KUM-pah-nees): Corporations that do at least some of their manufacturing in a foreign country and that operate with global priorities.

Many oil companies are multinational companies.

multiple listing service (MLS) (MUL-tih-pl LIST-ing SER-vis): A service from a group of real estate brokers who agree to share listings with one another.

When there is a sale from a multiple listing, the broker who sold the house shares the commission with the broker who listed it.

multitasking (MUL-ti-TASK-ing): A type of operating system that allows more than one program to run at the same time.

My new computer has the ability to do multitasking.

mutual fund (MU-chu-el fund): A portfolio of investments run by an investment firm.

Jason took his Christmas bonus and invested it in a mutual fund.

naked position (NA-ked po-ZISH-un): A very risky position in securities that is not hedged.

I know I put myself in a naked position with that purchase of stock, but I feel strongly that it will grow.

NASDAQ (National Association of Securities Dealers Automated Quotations) (NAZ-dak): An automated system of listing stock prices.

If you want to know the price of our stock at any time, just check NASDAQ.

national advertising (NAH-shun-el AD-ver-tize-ing): Advertising done by a company that is trying to sell its product nationwide.

Widgets Inc. launched a national advertising campaign with the slogan, "Widgets are wonderful."

national debt (NAH-shun-el det): The money owed by the federal government. The debt is in the form of Treasury bills, Treasury notes, and Treasury bonds.

> *The senator went on television and said the national debt is way too high.*

negative cash flow (NEG-ah-tiv cash flo): Spending more money than is received during an accounting period.

> *With the lawsuits and the breakdown of equipment and the strike, Widgets Inc. experienced a negative cash flow this quarter.*

negligence (NEG-lih-jens): A legal term for the failure to do the right thing in a particular circumstance.

> *The lawyer claimed, "It was negligence when Widgets Inc. put those dangerous widgets on the market."*

negligent manufacture (NEG-lih-jent man-u-FAK-chure): A charge made in a product liability suit against a manufacturer. When someone is injured by a product, such as a lawnmower, automobile, snowmobile, or whatever, they can sue the manufacturer for negligence.

> *Ron is suing Widgets Inc. for negligent manufacture because he broke both his legs while using its widget.*

negotiable (ne-GO-she-ah-bl): A set of conditions that is open for discussion when two parties are working on a deal.

> *Widgets Inc. and Stuff Company agreed on the price of the buyout, and the management structure of the new division is negotiable.*

nepotism (NEP-o-tizm): Favoritism given to family members of current employees when hiring or promoting employees.

> *Widgets Inc. was rampant with nepotism. Almost all of the top officers of the company are either Widgets or have married into the Widget family.*

net (net): The amount that is left after all proper deductions are made from the gross.

The way to figure net sales is to take gross sales and deduct allowances, discounts, and returns.

net profits (net PROF-its): The money earned by a business after all expenses have been deducted from total revenues.

Stuff Company had high revenues last year, but their net profits were very small. The company is selling a lot, but it's not making any money.

network (NET-werk): A system in which computers are linked together.

Jan is on the network at the university.

networking (NET-werk-ing): The deliberate act of befriending people for the purpose of doing business.

It always helps to give out a nice business card when networking.

net worth (net werth): Assets minus liabilities.

When Jane graduated from college, her net worth was minus $50,000. But she has worked a few years, paid off her college loans, and now her net worth is $500,000.

new money (nu MUN-e): New funding that a company gets from the issue of new long-term securities.

Widgets Inc. has some new money to fund its venture into Asia.

newsgroup (NUZE-grupe): A discussion and information area on the Internet for people who are interested in one specific subject.

Jerry is in a newsgroup for collectors of old Cleveland Indians' baseball cards.

New York Stock Exchange (NYSE) (new york stok ex-CHANJE): The biggest and oldest stock exchange in the United States.

Widgets Inc. is listed on the New York Stock Exchange.

next in, first out (NIFO) (next in first out): A method of recording the value of inventory in which profits and margins are figured from the cost of replacing an item rather than the historical cost of an item.

Widgets Inc. sold widgets for $50. The widgets cost $30 to make, but if the company needs to replace them with new widgets, they would cost $40 to make because of inflation. Using the NIFO method, gross profits are $10 per widget.

niche (nich): A small specialty market that often has little competition.

My grandfather told me to find my own niche and I would make a lot of money.

niche writer (nich RITE-er): An insurance company that develops a specialized knowledge about a certain type of coverage, or area, or demographic group of consumers.

Brenda found a niche writer for small, high-tech retail companies.

no-fault automobile insurance (no fault AU-to-mo-BELE in-SHURE-ens): Type of automobile insurance that will pay for any loss suffered by the insured without regard to who is at fault. The idea is to cut down on unnecessary lawsuits. No-fault insurance usually stays in effect until a loss exceeds a certain amount. When that happens, the door is only then open for lawsuits.

After my car and another skidded into each other in the snowstorm, no one tried very hard to find either of us at fault. After all, we both had no-fault automobile insurance, so fault didn't much matter in this minor fender bender.

no-load (no lode): A mutual fund that comes without a commission fee.

I invested in a no-load fund and it has grown quite a bit. All in all, it was a great deal.

nolo contendere (NO-lo kon-TEN-deh-re): A legal plea in court that means, "I do not want to fight or contend with the charge." Such a plea always brings a decision against the defendant, but it is not recognized in any other court as an admission of guilt.

John took a limo from his mansion to court, where he pled nolo contendere to embezzling $5 million from Widgets Inc.

nominal damages (NOM-ih-nel DAM-ejz): A very small award given in a legal case in which the defendant was legally wrong.

Michael sued the hamburger joint for $4 million because they put ketchup on his burger when he explicitly told them four times that he was allergic to ketchup. Since he never ate the burger and never actually got sick, he won only nominal damages of $1 plus the cost of the burger.

nonbearing wall (non-BEAR-ing wall): A wall in a building that is not a structural support for the building.

The wall between the den and the living room is a nonbearing wall that we could tear down to make the living room much bigger.

nonbusiness income (non-BIZ-ness IN-kum): A taxation term used to help figure the net operating loss deduction. Nonbusiness income is money that comes from dividends, interest, or capital gains that exceed capital losses.

The accountant said, "If you remove your nonbusiness income, which is large from all your dividends, you will see that you had quite a net operating loss."

nonconforming (non-kun-FORM-ing): A zoning term meaning a building or use that pre-existed a law banning such a building or use. Also called pre-existing condition.

> *There is a new zoning law in town calling for one-acre lots, but I bought a nonconforming lot that was subdivided years before the new law.*

noncontributory (non-kun-TRIB-u-to-re): A benefit plan for employees that is fully paid for by the employer.

> *My new job at Widgets Inc. is great. The company even has a non-contributory health plan. I don't have to pay a penny out of my paycheck.*

noncurrent asset (non-KUR-rent ASS-set): An asset that is not expected to be sold anytime soon.

> *Our factory building is a noncurrent asset.*

nondurable goods (non-DU-rah-bl goods): Goods that are not meant to last, such as food.

> *Newspapers are nondurable goods.*

nonprofit organization (non-PROF-it OR-gen-i-ZA-shun): A group that can exist without having to pay taxes. This organization are usually involved in some activity that benefits society, such as a charity, school, hospital, or church.

> *Save the Chipmunks is a nonprofit environmental organization.*

nonqualified plan (non-KWAL-ih-fide plan): An employee benefit plan in which employers do not receive a tax deduction for their contributions on behalf of employees. Such a plan allows the employer to distribute benefits, and the cost to employees is often less than for qualified plans.

> *Stuff Company has a nonqualified plan that doesn't cost a lot, but I'm worried what will happen if someone in my family gets sick.*

nonvoting stock (non-VOTE-ing stok): Stock that has financial value but does not give the holder any right to vote on corporate matters or the election of officers.

I own nonvoting stock in Widgets Inc. I don't care about their silly corporate intrigue and infighting, I merely want higher stock prices.

normal cost (NOR-mel kost): The average annual cost of a product. The price of something is checked monthly for a year and then averaged out to guard against seasonal changes.

Normal costs for a product include materials, labor, and overhead averaged out over a year.

normal distribution (NOR-mel dis-trih-BU-shun): A bell-shaped probability distribution graph that shows the mean (the peak of the bell) and the standard deviation.

The president of the company wants to know the normal distribution of the age of our customers.

normal wear and tear (NOR-mel wair and tair): Expected depreciation due to aging and deterioration of a product.

Of course that car went down in value, because normal wear and tear brings the value down some.

North American Free Trade Agreement (NAFTA) (nafta): A trade agreement signed by the U.S., Canada, and Mexico and passed by the U.S. in 1993 under President Clinton. The agreement, which phases out tariffs, is designed to encourage free trade between the countries.

Many union workers are opposed to NAFTA because they think they will lose jobs to Mexico, where wages are much lower.

NOW account (now uh-COUNT): It stands for Negotiable Order of Withdrawal account. It is a checking account that bears interest and usually has a limit on the number of checks that can be written from it within a month.

Jan took her Christmas bonus and put it in a NOW account that she would access only to pay her mortgage once a month.

number cruncher (NUM-ber KRUNCH-er): A person whose work involves spending time manipulating numbers.

I don't understand. The boss was really sarcastic when he told me to send my budget to accounting and see what the number crunchers up there think about it.

objective (OB-jek-TIV): A final goal.

The president was incredulous when he spoke to the intern. "Is your objective to see how much you can tick me off?" he asked.

object-oriented (OB-jekt O-re-ent-ed): A way of organizing software so that the actual task one wants to accomplish is the command, rather than needing a series of commands to get to that point.

Smartypants Software is touting its new object-oriented accounting software.

obliger (o-BLI-jer): A person who obligates himself to another.

I received advance money for that project, so now I am an obliger until I finish it.

obsolescence (ob-so-LES-sens): The changing of the market for a product to the point that the product becomes useless. With obsolescence, the product still works but there is no need for it.

Software from fifteen years ago still works but it is so outdated it faces virtual obsolescence.

occupancy rate (OK-ku-pen-se rate): The percentage of income that is received from occupants in a boarding facility, such as a hotel or inn, compared to what would be received if the facility were completely filled.

> *The occupancy rate for the skyscraper owned by Widgets Inc. is only 70 percent. It dropped significantly when the recession started.*

occupational hazard (OK-ku-PA-shun-el HAZ-erd): Type of hazard from an occupation that cannot be eliminated and is considered a by-product of the work.

> *Falling to your death is an occupational hazard associated with tightrope walking.*

Occupational Safety and Health Administration (OSHA) (O-shah): The federal office that is responsible for the safety of the workplace.

> *After Mandy was hurt on the job, she complained to OSHA about conditions at Widgets Inc.*

offering price (OFF-fer-ing prise): The price of securities offered for sale.

> *Widgets Inc. is offering new stock this week but the company hasn't revealed the offering price.*

offsetting error (off-SET-ing ER-rur): An accounting error that cancels out an opposite accounting error.

> *The company overstated how much was received from one customer but understated how much was received from another. These were offsetting errors since the amount of the errors was the same.*

off the books (off the books): A transaction that is not recorded in any accounting books. Such transactions usually involve cash and are done for the purpose of hiding any evidence from taxation.

> *John got an off-the-books job when he was home from college for the summer.*

online (on-LINE): When one computer has made a successful connection with another through a network or telephone line.

I went online last night to look up information on the history of the company, Widgets Inc.

OPEC (Organization of Petroleum Exporting Countries) (O-pek): Cartel of countries that produce and export petroleum. The organization, at times, has tried to control the world's oil supply and prices.

The president was worried when he heard that OPEC is planning a meeting next month in the hope of organizing a price hike.

open distribution (O-pen dis-trih-BU-shun): When different dealers in the same region distribute the same product and compete with one another.

In the biggest cities, Widgets Inc. has found it makes sense to go with open distribution.

open shop (O-pen shop): A business that employs people whether or not they are in a union.

John used to work in a union shop until he was laid off, and now he works for an open shop. His wages are lower but he doesn't have to pay union dues.

operating expense (op-er-A-ting ex-PENS): The cost of maintaining property, including taxes, insurance, and utilities.

The operating expense on this old building is very high.

operating system (op-er-A-ting SIS-tem): The program that runs a computer and which runs other programs.

The operating system on my computer is MS-DOS.

operations research (op-er-A-shuns RE-surch): Research of repetitive operations using mathematical computer models to find more efficient ways of doing things.

> *The folks in operations research have concluded that if we put the back on the widget first, instead of the front, it could save time and expense.*

opinion leader (o-PIN-yun LEDE-er): A person who, by virtue of his position, popularity, or some other reason, has been shown to speak for others.

> *The rock star Johnny Lightning is considered an opinion leader for thirteen-year-old boys. If we can get him to say our widgets are great, half of the thirteen-year-old boys in America will want a widget.*

opportunity cost (op-pur-TU-nih-te kost): When there is more than one option, the opportunity cost is the rate of return there would be if the best course option were chosen.

> *The president of the company wants to know the opportunity cost of manufacturing widgets in Bulgaria versus making them in Michigan.*

option (OP-chun): The right to purchase something within a given period of time. It is not an obligation, and the person who has the option pays an agreed-upon price to hold the option for the time period. If the option is not exercised by the end of the time period, the person who holds the option forfeits the money paid for it.

> *Jane has an option to buy stock in Widgets Inc.*

oral contract (O-rel KON-trakt): Contract that is not in writing.

> *I have an oral contract with Widgets Inc. to start work there as an engineer.*

order-point system (OR-der point SIS-tem): A system of inventory that automatically reorders when inventory levels drop to a certain point.

Widgets Inc. uses an order-point system for all of its widget parts, in order to be sure it never has to shut down the production line.

ordinary income (OR-dih-nar-e IN-kum): Income that is not from capital gains. Such income, including dividends, wages, and interest, is subject to normal income taxes, while capital gains taxes are lower than normal income taxes.

Carol earned a lot of money last year but not much of it was ordinary income. She sold a lot of inherited property, meaning she had to pay capital gains taxes.

organization chart (OR-gen-i-ZA-shun chart): A diagram showing the lines of responsibility within an organization.

If you draw an organization chart, you will see the problem with Widgets Inc. Over on one side you have marketing, who are making decisions with no supervision, and on the other side you have research and development, who are answering to any of a dozen managers who all want a product for their department.

organizational behavior (OR-gen-i-ZA-shun-el be-HAV-yur): The study of how people behave inside an organization.

Organizational behavior includes such categories as leadership, trust, negotiating, decision making, and career control.

original cost (o-RIJ-ih-nel kost): How much it costs to acquire an item.

The original cost of the part for my car's engine was $60, but my local mechanic charged me $240 for it.

origination fee (o-rij-ih-NA-shun fe): The fee that a lender charges to a borrower to cover the costs of a loan. This fee often includes a sales commission.

When you are figuring the costs of your loan, don't forget the origination fee.

OS/2 (o-s-tu): An operating program that runs on the IBM PC that can run more than one program at once.

I like having OS/2 because it allows me to run my word processing and my spreadsheet at the same time.

other income (UTH-er IN-kum): Income reported on a profit-and-loss statement that does not come from the normal course of business. This category includes interest from investments, profits from selling things other than inventory, and a profit on the foreign exchange.

When Sue went to Mexico for two months and then came back, she had earned a lot of money on the foreign exchange and her company recorded it as other income.

other people's money (OPM) (UTH-er PE-pls MUN-e): Borrowed money to finance an investment.

Widgets Inc. built a new factory in Bulgaria with OPM.

outlet (OUT-let): A retail store run by a manufacturer for the express purpose of selling merchandise from the manufacturer—often merchandise that is irregular, overstocked, or out of season.

My grandma likes shopping at the outlets because she can always find good deals.

out-of-pocket expenses (out of POK-et ex-PENS-es): The use of personal funds to pay for personal or business expenses.

Stuart always has some small, out-of-pocket expenses for every project.

outside director (OUT-side dih-REKT-ur): A person who is on a company's board of directors but is not an employee of the company.

The president of the company likes to get feedback from the outside directors because he says they are unbiased.

outsourcing (out-SORS-ing): Having a part of your operation fulfilled by an outside company.

Widgets Inc. is outsourcing all of its accounting to another firm.

overage (O-ver-ej): Too much of something.

The company has an overage of rear widget parts but not enough front widget parts.

overbooked (O-ver-bookd): When a ferry boat, airline, hotel, or some other business takes too many reservations.

Jim's flight to Los Angeles was overbooked, so he was bumped and had to catch a later flight.

overdraft (O-ver-draft): When a check is written against an account that does not have enough money to cover the amount of the check.

When Frank's old college roommate came to visit, Frank wrote a check to cover a night on the town. Unfortunately, his paycheck had not yet cleared and the check Frank wrote was an overdraft.

overkill (O-ver-kil): Expensive advertising campaign that is memorable to consumers, but memorable in a bad way.

Donna said, "I hate those Widgets Inc. commercials. They are on all the time and they are really obnoxious. It's overkill. I'll never buy a widget."

overrun (O-ver-run): A production run that is larger than what is needed.

Widgets Inc. had an overrun of its older-model widgets because it wanted to use up excess inventory before it switched its production line exclusively to high-tech widgets.

over the counter (OTC) (O-ver the COUNT-er): A stock that is not listed on the exchange but is still traded.

Stock in Stuff Company is over the counter.

overtime (O-ver-time): Time that is worked in excess of a normal forty-hour work week. Overtime is paid at 1½ times the regular hourly rate.

Pete was happy to get a job at Widgets Inc. because the company told him he could work all the overtime that he wants.

owner (OWN-er): One who has a title, whether he has possession or not.

Marty is the owner of this motorcycle. He just lets me ride it.

pacesetter (PASE-SET-er): Something that blazes trails in an industry and then is widely copied.

The new high-tech widget is the pacesetter for the industry. All the competition are scrambling to come up with their own version.

package code (PACK-ej kode): An identification code put on a direct-mail package.

When Sue called Widgets Inc. to tell them she received the wrong color widgets, the company asked her to tell them the package code.

package design (PACK-ej de-ZINE): Working out details of color, size, form, convenience, labeling, and anything else that has to do with how a package looks, holds up, or works.

Stephanie in marketing insists that the most important part of developing a new product is package design, because the package is what the customer first sees.

packaged goods (PACK-ejd goods): Goods that are packaged by manufacturers and then sold to consumers through retail stores.

Cigarettes and audiocassettes are both packaged goods.

packaging list (PACK-ej-ing list): A document that shows all the contents of a container. The list is put in the container.

The first thing Walter does when he opens a package that arrives at the warehouse is to check the packaging list and compare it to the contents of the package.

padding (PAD-ing): Putting excess, untrue charges into an expense account.

John asked the waitress to double the amount of his receipt. "I'm padding my expense account," he said.

pagination (paj-ih-NA-shun): A computer process of dividing a document into pages.

When Beth writes her novels, she just sets the pagination command and her page breaks are set.

paid-in capital (pade in KAP-ih-tel): Money paid for stock as opposed to money that is earned.

Widgets Inc. experienced a jump in paid-in capital because of its recent stock offering.

panic (PAN-ik): A sudden, unreasoning fear in the market that can make investors act harshly.

When Widgets Inc. president, Edgar Widget, announced he was selling off all of his shares in his company, it caused a minor panic in the widget market. Prices fell for three days before stabilizing.

parallel processing (PAR-el-lel PROS-es-ing): When a computer does two or more functions at the same time.

Dan always brags about his new computer's ability to do parallel processing.

parameter (pah-RAM-e-ter): A set quantity.

How many sample customers do you want us to quote in our report? How many pages do you want? Give us some parameters.

parent company (PAR-ent KUM-pah-ne): A company that owns the voting stock in its subsidiaries, and therefore controls those companies.

Stuff Company manufactures parts for widgets and is owned by Widgets Inc. Widgets Inc. is the parent company in that relationship.

parliamentary procedure (par-lah-MEN-tah-re pro-SE-dure): Formal rules for how a meeting should be run.

Our board meetings always start with the intention of following parliamentary procedure, but they inevitably degenerate into uncontrollable shouting matches.

partial liquidation (PAR-shel lik-wih-DA-shun): Distributions to shareholders. These distributions may qualify as capital gains.

When there is partial liquidation, a shareholder receives a number of distributions.

participation loan (par-tis-ih-PA-shun lone): A loan made by one bank but backed by other banks.

> *The president of Widgets Inc. said, "My local bank was the lead lender in the participation loan that got my factory built and brought in 250 jobs."*

participative leadership (par-TIS-ih-pa-tiv LEDE-er-ship): Management style in which workers are encouraged to give opinions and participate in meetings where decisions are made.

> *Bob loves working at Widgets Inc. because the participative leadership really inspires him.*

partnership (PART-ner-ship): Business relationship between two or more people who agree to share their talents, profits, and losses in specific portions.

> *The Widget, Wazzit, and Wherzit Law Firm is a partnership.*

par value (par VAL-u): The face value of a bond, or how much it pays at maturity.

> *The par value of the five-year bond is $10,000.*

passive activity (PAS-siv ak-TIV-ih-te): An investing activity, such as renting, in which the investor does not actively participate.

> *Income that comes from rental activity income that comes from a passive activity.*

password (PASS-wurd): A secret combination of letters and numbers that is used to identify a user to a computer or computer network.

> *Before I log on to AOL, I have to give my password.*

past service benefit (past SERV-is BEN-eh-fit): A credit given in a new pension plan. The credit is for an employee's service with a company before the pension plan was established.

The amount Carol was given for a past service benefit wasn't great, but it was better than nothing.

patent (PAT-ent): A protection right granted to an inventor. The patent does not allow anyone else to market the invention for a specified time period.

Widgets Inc. was just granted a patent for its new high-tech widget.

patent holder (PAT-ent HOLDE-er): One who owns a patent.

Jonathan Widget was the original patent holder on the widget, invented in 1907 in Dayton, Ohio.

paternalism (pah-TER-nel-ism): Management style that some snicker at because it puts employees on a lower level than management. With paternalism, management makes all decisions for employees.

Harry complained that Widgets Inc. was run by paternalism because the company pushed his career in a direction he didn't want to go, and because the company even told him what color of car to get—red.

payable (PA-ah-bl): The amount owed.

Our accounts payable is pretty high. I hope some checks come in so we can pay some of those bills.

paycheck/payday (PA-chek/PA-da): A paycheck is the instrument of compensation one receives for work. The day one is paid is called payday.

The only good part about working for Widgets Inc. is when I receive my paycheck on payday.

payment in kind (PA-ment in kinde): An exchange of a value for an agreed-upon equal value.

Joe the plumber fixed Ann the advertising lady's faucet. She then wrote a slogan for television ads. They both agreed it was payment in kind.

payout (PA-out): The amount of money that must be raised from an advertising campaign to pay for the campaign itself.

The last advertising campaign run for Widgets Inc. was so horrendous it didn't even reach payout.

PC-compatible (pe-se kum-PAT-ih-bl): A computer that can do the same things and run the same software as an IBM PC.

Rosemary found a small company called Electrogadgets that makes a really nice PC-compatible.

peer review (peer re-VU): An inspection of the work of one CPA or of an accounting firm by another CPA or firm.

Every time the CPA at Widgets Inc. goes under peer review, she gets nervous.

pension fund (PEN-shun fund): A fund set up for the retirement of employees. The fund is paid into by employees and the employer and is managed by an outside firm.

One of the things Nancy likes about working at Widgets Inc. is the pension fund.

Pentium processor (PENT-e-um PROS-ses-ur): The brand name of the very fast Intel 586 microprocessor chip.

My new computer came with a Pentium processor. I can't wait to get it going and see how fast it really is.

peon (PE-on): An employee with trivial duties who is looked down upon.

> *When you work at Widgets Inc., management goes out of its way to treat you like a peon.*

people intensive (PE-pl in-TEN-siv): A workplace that needs a lot of people in order to succeed. The kind of work that cannot be automated.

> *Designing software is people intensive.*

per capita (per KAP-ih-tah): A calculation of a number that applies equally to each person in a population.

> *The average per capita salary in my small town is $17,000 per year.*

per diem (per DE-em): Payment by the day, or expenses paid by the day.

> *Sam went to work for Widgets Inc. on a per diem basis, while his brother Stan received a per diem allowance of $50 for each of the three days of his upcoming sales trip.*

performance appraisal (per-FORM-ens ap-PRAIS-EL): A specific way of rating an employee by setting up objective criteria.

> *When Alex saw his performance appraisal, he strongly disagreed with some parts of it.*

performance audit (per-FORM-ens AW-dit): An examination of the way a specific action is performed within a company.

> *Widgets Inc. is conducting a performance audit of the final stage of the production line.*

performance bond (per-FORM-ens bond): A bond put up by a contractor to a local government that guarantees the work will meet all zoning requirements.

The planning commission wants a performance bond as a condition of it granting permission for the new subdivision.

peripherals (peh-RIF-er-els): Extras added onto a computer system.

My computer has a few peripherals, including a CD-ROM drive and a printer.

perpetual insurance (per-peh-CHU-el in-SHURE-ens): Insurance coverage in which a single premium payment pays for the insurance of property, with no time limit.

Edgar Widget, the president of Widgets Inc., has perpetual insurance on each of his five mansions.

perpetuity (per-peh-TU-ih-te): Forever.

After Jonathan Widget retired, he received a salary in perpetuity until he died.

perquisite (perk): Fringe benefit that an employee gets for working someplace. You get perks in addition to wages.

The best perk of working at Widgets Inc. is the free widgets.

per se (per sa): Inherently.

Edgar Widget, the president of Widgets Inc., is a millionaire per se.

personal exemption (PER-sun-el ex-EMP-shun): Taxpayers are allowed a personal exemption deduction for themselves, their spouse, and their dependents.

When Joe's triplets were born, it gave him three new personal exemptions.

personal information manager (PIM) (PER-sun-el in-for-MA-shun): An electronic daily planner on a computer.

The first thing Amy does every morning when she gets in is to check her PIM. And the last thing she does every night before she goes home is to make entries in her PIM for the next day.

personal property (PER-sun-el PROP-er-te): Property that is not permanently attached to a piece of land.

My toaster and my automobile are both personal property.

personnel department (per-sun-NEL de-PART-ment): Department within a company that deals with personnel issues.

Matthew visited the personnel department with a question about his vacation time.

perspective (per-SPEK-tiv): The point of view of someone. In other words, how one sees something both visually and perceives it based on personal experience.

The art director said that all advertisements need to consider the perspective of their audience.

persuasion (per-SWA-zhun): A successful attempt at changing someone's opinion and getting that person to take action.

"Sometimes the best form of persuasion is to just tell the truth," said the president of Widgets Inc.

Peter Principle (PE-ter PRIN-sih-pl): Theory that all people rise to their level of incompetence in work.

Randy was the best salesman in all of Widgets Inc., so the company made him sales manager, and he was terrible. Randy certainly proved the Peter Principle.

petitioner (peh-TISH-un-er): A party that is requesting a court to take an action.

Sophie is the petitioner for an injunction to stop Widgets Inc. from beginning to build its new factory.

petrodollar (PET-ro-DOL-ler): A dollar deposited in a Western bank by an oil-producing nation that earned the dollar from the sale of oil.

I have a strong bank. There are a lot of petrodollars in it.

petty cash (PET-te kash): A small fund of cash that is readily available to pay for small, miscellaneous expenses.

The company bought a birthday cake for Jan out of petty cash.

phantom stock plan (FAN-tum stok plan): A compensation plan that is not stock but is based on the stock price of the employer.

Every employee on the factory floor knew the price of stock of Widgets Inc. because the company offered a phantom stock plan.

photocopier (FO-to-KOP-e-er): A machine that photographically duplicates documents.

Run that report through the photocopier. We need twelve copies for tomorrow's meeting.

physical examination (FIZ-ik-el ex-am-ih-NA-shun): In-person, physical inspection of an object.

After the third crash in a month, the government ordered a physical examination of all the planes of Cheapo Airlines.

physical verification (FIZ-ik-el VER-ih-fih-KA-shun): Physical examination of something in order to count and/or record the amount and type of items to compare it with a list.

Someone in the Bighugefaceless Store warehouse always does a physical verification that there are fifty widgets in every fifty-pack of widgets.

picketing (PIK-et-ing): Marching in a public place, often near a place of employment, to protest something or to voice a grievance or a reason for a strike.

People who are picketing frequently carry signs.

piecework (pese wurk): Work that pays by the unit produced.

The work Beth does for the PR agency is essentially piecework, since she gets paid a set rate for each event she hosts and for each release she writes.

pie chart (pi chart): A graph in which a circle represents a whole unit, and pie-shaped pieces represent parts of the whole.

If you look at this pie chart of sales by widget companies, you will see that Widgets Inc. has more than half the sales.

pigeonholed (PIJ-un-holed): Putting something or someone aside and leaving it there in a forgotten state.

The boss pigeonholed my last project.

piggyback loan (PIG-ge-bak lone): A construction loan that is accompanied by a commitment for a permanent loan.

We have a piggyback loan for the construction of our house and then the mortgage on the new house.

pink slip (pink slip): A symbolic term for being told you are laid off. Often, layoff slips have been pink.

Ted went home all stressed out because his company had given out 500 pink slips and he didn't get one. All that he knew was that the company would be giving out another 2,000 pink slips next week.

plaintiff (PLANE-tiff): One who sues.

Joe Miller is the plaintiff in the suit against Widgets Inc. His wife died when a widget caught on fire, and now he is suing Widgets Inc.

plan B (plan be): A backup plan in case the primary plan doesn't work.

The boss said, "Okay, that didn't work. Let's try plan B."

planned economy (pland e-KON-o-me): Situation in which the government manipulates the economy more than the free market does.

Communist countries are planned economies, at least in theory.

planning (PLAN-ing): Determining the step-by-step process that is needed to reach a goal.

The company has a planning meeting this afternoon to come up with a strategy for our new product.

plowback (PLOW-bak): Investing earnings back in the business rather than paying out higher dividends.

Stuff Company is young and growing, so it is going to plow back its earnings into the business.

point (point): A charge by a lender to pay for the expenses of a mortgage. A single point is equal to 1 percent of the entire loan. For instance, one point on a $100,000 loan is $1,000.

Mickey and Sue took out a $150,000 mortgage and were charged two points in fees. Their fees were $3,000.

point-of-purchase display (point of PUR-ches dis-PLA): A product information display that is located in a prime area in a retail store.

The state lottery has a point-of-purchase display filled with brochures and slips for tickets, right near the machine for tickets.

point-of-sale (point of sale): Retail system of tracking sales figures. A computer terminal is put in specific areas of the store. This adds a convenience for the customer, and instant inventory control for the store.

The store manager liked the point-of-sale system because it made his job of reordering very easy.

point-to-point protocol (PPP) (point to point PRO-to-kol): One method that computers can use to connect to each other.

> *You cannot go on the Internet until you establish a PPP connection.*

policy (POL-ih-se): A policy of a company is a governing principle. Or . . . An insurance policy is the printed agreement that puts insurance coverage into place.

> *It is the policy of Widgets Inc. to have each employee take a lie detector test. Or . . . Elaine has taken out an insurance policy on her new house.*

political action committee (PAC) (po-LIT-ih-kel AK-chun kum-MIT-te): A fund that is set up for the purpose of donating money to political causes.

> *Almost every politician complains about PAC money, but every politician wants PAC money.*

Ponzi scheme (PON-ze skeme): An illegal investment scheme in which money from new investors is used to pay existing investors interest and principal.

> *My old high school classmate, Jimmy Swindles, was arrested for running a Ponzi scheme aimed at elderly widows.*

pooling-of-interests (POOL-ing of IN-ter-ests): Method of accounting used when two businesses combine. The assets and liabilities of both companies are added together.

> *Widgets Inc., which is taking over Stuff Company, is doing pooling of interests.*

portfolio (port-FO-le-o): The group of all securities owned by an investor.

> *Many investors think it is best to have a diversified portfolio.*

portfolio income (port-FO-le-o IN-kum): A taxation term for money that is earned from investments, including interest and dividends. It does not include money earned from passive activity such as renting.

I had a high portfolio income this year.

portfolio manager (port-FO-le-o MAN-ah-jer): A professional who takes care of a portfolio for a company or individual.

Jane called her portfolio manager for some advice on what to do with her stock from Widgets Inc.

positive cash flow (POZ-ih-tiv kash-flo): Cash flow before adding an income tax refund or deducting income tax payments.

Widgets Inc. has a nice positive cash flow, but the company expects to pay a lot in taxes.

possession (po-ZESH-un): Something that is in one's control and that one has a claimed controlling authority over.

This antique widget is my most prized possession.

post (poste): The transfer of a debit or credit from a journal to the right account in a ledger.

The accountant is going to post the debit from the purchase of new equipment.

posting (POSTE-ing): Physically listing something.

I heard that the company will be posting that job notice next week.

power of attorney (POW-er of at-TUR-ne): The authority that one person is granted to be allowed to take certain actions on behalf of another.

After Joe was injured in the automobile accident, he granted power of attorney to his sister, Teresa.

power surge (POW-er surj): A sudden rise in electric voltage that can be dangerous to computers.

It is important to get a surge protector for your computer because almost every electrical outlet is subject to getting a power surge.

practical capacity (PRAK-tih-kul cah-PAS-ih-te): The busiest a factory can be while still being efficient. Also called maximum practical capacity.

It doesn't make sense for the company to take on any new orders because the factory is already running at practical capacity.

precious metals (PRESH-us MET-els): Valuable metals that are very liquid and have an international market. These metals, such as gold and silver, have advantages and disadvantages as an investment. They are very liquid and they are a hedge against inflation, but they tend to go down in value during good times and there is a high storage cost.

Winston always owns some precious metals as a hedge against his risky plays of the stock market.

predatory pricing (PRED-ah-to-re PRISE-ing): Lowering prices with the intention of making it imposssible for smaller companies to compete. Once those companies fold, the idea is to then raise prices.

Widgets Inc. has been accused of predatory pricing in the widget market.

pre-emptive rights (pre-EMP-tiv rites): Rights given to existing stockholders to get the first opportunity to buy any new issues of a stock.

As a stockholder with Widgets Inc., Sue had pre-emptive rights to buy the company's new issue.

pre-existing condition (pre-ex-IST-ing kun-DIH-shun): A zoning term meaning a building or use that pre-existed prior to a law banning such a building or use. Also called nonconforming use of pre-existing condition.

> *There is a new zoning law in town calling for one-acre lots, but I bought a lot that was subdivided years before the new law. Therefore it is legal because of the pre-existing condition.*

preferential rehiring (pref-er-EN-shul re-HIRE-ing): Provision in the Civil Rights Act of 1964 in which employers can be required to rehire employees who had suffered discrimination. In such a case, the employer can be required to pay back pay to the employee.

> *Widgets Inc., found guilty of job discrimination, was told to do some preferential rehiring of two-dozen minority employees.*

preferred stock (pre-FERD stok): Stock that is a safe investment, and has a guaranteed dividend.

> *Beth owns preferred stock in Widgets Inc. because she doesn't like risk.*

premises (PREM-is-es): Land and any buildings on that land.

> *After Fred was fired, he was told he had ten minutes to get off of company premises.*

premium (PRE-me-um): The amount of money that is paid for insurance.

> *The president of Stuff Company was concerned that the premium he is paying for insurance keeps going up, even though the company has never had an accident. He called the insurance company and was told that his business, the widget business, was considered one of the most dangerous in the world.*

premium bond (PRE-me-um bond): A bond that sells for more than its face value.

> *Dennis has invested in a premium bond.*

prepaid (pre-PADE): A bill that is paid in advance.

I have a prepaid calling card to use for long-distance phone calls.

prerequisite (pre-REK-wih-sit): A condition that must be met before an action can occur.

A physical examination is a prerequisite for getting heath insurance from some companies.

prerogative (pre-ROG-ah-tiv): An indisputable right.

It is the president of Widgets Inc.'s prerogative to have all the widgets that he wants.

presentation (pres-en-TA-shun): A formal informational presentment of a plan of action that often includes charts and a discussion.

John is nervous because he has to give a presentation tomorrow.

present value (PRES-ent VAL-u): Current value of a future payment.

Widgets Inc. will receive a payment of $100,000 in five years. The present value of that future payment is $65,000 if interest rates stay the same.

president (PRES-ih-dent): The highest-ranking official in a company after the chairman of the board or, if used, the CEO. The president is appointed by the board of directors.

Larry Leader is the new president of Widgets Inc.

press kit (pres kit): A package of information sent out to the media in the hope of getting a story done or of clarifying information.

Widgets Inc. sent out 500 press kits when the company announced its new high-tech widget.

prestige pricing (pres-TEZHE PRISE-ing): Pricing policy designed to attract upscale customers by not stocking any low-priced items.

> *Widgets Inc. has gone with prestige pricing of its new high-tech widget.*

preventive care (pre-VENT-tive kair): An approach to health care in which a person is monitored by things such as regular physical examinations instead of merely waiting for the patient to get sick and then responding.

> *My new HMO is very big on preventive care. Every year, it schedules a physical examination for me as well as extensive blood work.*

price (prise): How much something costs.

> *The price of a loaf of bread is $1.09.*

price fixing (prise FIX-ing): Illegal collaboration between companies to raise or lower prices of a commodity.

> *Widgets Inc. and its main competitor, Stuff Company, have been accused by federal authorities of price fixing.*

price scanner (prise SKAN-er): A computer system that optically reads bar codes on products and inputs the information into a cash register and inventory system.

> *The clerk ran my widgets under the price scanner.*

price support (prise sup-PORT): Government policy of supporting certain industries such as agriculture by guaranteeing a certain price for a product. If the market price drops below that guaranteed price, the government makes up the difference.

> *Farmers in Nebraska are happy for the price support on corn.*

price war (prise war): When competing companies continually slash prices and try to offer customers the lowest price. A price war can be a bonanza for consumers but financially difficult for businesses.

All the gas stations in my town are having a price war on their premium gasoline prices.

pricing above/below the market (PRISE-ing ah-BUV/be-LO the MARket): Pricing strategy in which companies either try to appeal to a luxury market by pricing high and offering exceptional service, or try to appeal to a lower market by pricing really low.

Widgets Inc is pricing its regular widgets below market, but for its new high-tech widget it is pricing it above the market.

pricing decision (PRISE-ing de-SIZH-un): Decision made on how much to charge for a product.

Widgets Inc. has a pricing decision for its new high-tech widget, which it will put on the market in three months.

prima facie (PRI-mah FAH-she-ah): Adequate enough to establish as fact on first glance.

Ted's police uniform is prima facie evidence that he is a policeman.

prime rate (prime rate): Interest rate charged to the customers of a bank who have the best credit. It is used as a reference point for other loan rates given by the bank.

Sue received a loan at 2 percent over the prime rate.

principal (PRIN-sih-pel): The amount of money borrowed in a loan, not including the interest that is accrued.

The principal of my mortgage is $75,000, but after thirty years I will have paid more than $200,000 in principal and interest.

printer (PRINT-er): The machine connected to a computer that prints documents. There are many kinds of printers, including laser printers, inkjet printers, and dot matrix printers.

Ann is looking to buy a new printer so she can do some high-quality publishing.

priority (pri-OR-ih-te): The right to be paid first in a bankruptcy proceeding.

The mortgage holder on the Stuff Company factory has priority in getting reimbursed in the bankruptcy proceeding of the company.

prior period adjustment (PRI-or PE-re-ud): Financial transaction, involving either revenue or expenses, that is applicable to a previous accounting period.

The accounting office made a prior period adjustment to last quarter's books because of an accounting error that was just discovered.

privately held company (PRI-vet-le held KUM-pah-ne): A company owned by a few people. Such a company does not have stock that is sold on the open market.

Stuff Company is a privately held company. It is owned by three members of the Stuff family.

privatization (PRI-vet-ti-ZA-shun): The process a public company undergoes when buying back its stock to become a private company again. Or . . . The process of government property being transferred into private ownership.

Widgets Inc. is undergoing a privatization by buying back its stock. Or . . . In eastern European countries, there has been a flurry of privatization since the fall of communism.

probationary employee (pro-BA-shun-air-e em-PLOY-e): A new employee who is on probation for a certain period of time. During that time, employment is considered an experiment and the employee can be dismissed any time during the probationary period because the employee does not yet have any rights of seniority.

Joan is a probationary employee at Widgets Inc. Her probationary period ends in six months.

process division (PROS-ess dih-VIZH-un): Management strategy of dividing work by tasks and making each task a division in the company.

At Widgets Inc., there is process division among workers assembling front widget parts, those assembling rear widget parts, and those who are doing final assembly of the two completed parts.

processor (PROS-ess-ur): The part of a computer that can manipulate data.

The technician said the problem with her computer was that she had a faulty processor.

procurement (pro-KURE-ment): Acquiring goods that are needed to run a business.

The president complained that the company is paying too much for supplies. "We need to do a better job of procurement," he said.

Prodigy (PROD-ih-je): A commercial online service.

Betty has signed on with Prodigy because she likes the things that are available for her children.

producer goods (pro-DUSE-er goods): The equipment needed to produce goods.

This new widget-making machine is just one example of the money Widgets Inc. has poured into producer goods in the last year.

product (PROD-ukt): The final result of the production process, the thing a company makes and sells.

Widgets Inc. makes many products, but its number-one seller is the standard-size widget.

production (pro-DUK-shun): Organized process of making, storing, and transporting goods.

The president of Widgets Inc. expressed concern that production at the company is too slow.

productivity (pro-duk-TIV-ih-te): Relationship between the number of units produced and the units of time for labor.

The president of Widgets Inc. noticed that the new widget-making machine has brought much greater productivity from his workers.

product liability (PROD-ukt li-ah-BIL-ih-te): The responsibility of a manufacturer to not make dangerous products. If a company knowingly puts a defective product on the market, it can be held liable for injuries it causes.

Widgets Inc. is very leery of product liability suits and inspects every production run of its widgets.

profit (PROF-it): Money earned from the sale of a product that exceeds the amount paid to make it.

Widgets Inc. gets a nice profit on each of its widgets. That is how it made the Fortune 500 list of top companies.

profit-and-loss statement (PROF-it and loss STATE-ment): Accounting statement summarizing expenses and revenues during an accounting period.

The president of Widgets Inc. spent the day studying last quarter's profit-and-loss statement, trying to figure out why the company had its worst quarter in a decade.

profit center (PROF-it SEN-ter): Part of a business that is profitable on its own accord.

> *Widgets Inc. has three profit centers: the high-tech widget division, the standard widget division, and the widget repair division.*

profit motive (PROF-it MO-tiv): A desire to make money on a business venture.

> *If there is not a profit motive for an activity, losses are tax deductible only up to the point of total income.*

profit-sharing plan (PROF-it SHAR-ing plan): Plan for employees to receive a portion of the company's profits.

> *Nancy loves the fact that Widgets Inc. has a profit-sharing plan, because the company has been profitable for fifty consecutive years.*

program (PRO-gram): A set of instructions that tells a computer what to do.

> *This company is running a new accounting program that is efficient and easy to use.*

progressive tax (pro-GRES-siv tax): A tax system, such as in the U.S., in which those who earn more money are charged a higher percentage of taxes than those who earn less money.

> *Many people like the progressive tax system because they think it is the fairest way of taxing citizens.*

progress payments (PROG-ress PA-ments): Payments given to a contractor as the contractor completes each stage of a construction project.

> *The contractor on Jesse's house is due for a progress payment now that the foundation has been poured.*

projection (pro-JEK-shun): An educated guess about what the future holds.

> *The marketing department has made a very ambitious sales projection for the upcoming year.*

promissory note (PROM-is-so-re note): A formal, written promise to pay a specific sum of money by a certain date.

> *Dale borrowed $2,000 from his parents and wrote them a promissory note to pay back the money within a year.*

promotion (pro-MO-shun): Moving to a better job. Or . . . The effort expended to sell a product.

> *John received a promotion to vice president. Or . . . Widgets Inc. is running a special "Buy one, get one free" promotion on its high-tech widgets.*

prompt (prompt): Something that appears on a computer screen that tells a user where to input a command.

> *I input my commands for DOS at the C prompt, which looks like this: "C:"*

proprietary fund (pro-PRI-eh-tar-e fund): A mutual fund managed by a bank, rather than an outside fund that the bank sells.

> *Jenny invested in a proprietary fund from her bank because she always liked the service the bank has given her and she has grown to trust the bank's judgment.*

prorate (pro-RATE): To divide a bill or payment proportionally between a buyer and seller.

> *When Bill sold his house to Jane, they had to prorate the taxes that Bill had already paid for the year.*

pros and cons (prose and kons): The positive and negative aspects of a specific situation.

> *Karen is weighing the pros and cons of switching jobs. On the plus side, she would make more money. On the negative side, she would be leaving a job that she loves for an unknown situation.*

prospect (PROS-pekt): A potential employee.

> *Widgets Inc. is visiting Harvard this week to seek prospects for its management program.*

prospectus (pro-SPEK-tus): A formal written description of a company that is putting stock up for sale. The prospectus is the actual offer to sell stock, and it is full of pertinent information about the company.

> *Widgets Inc. is putting out a new issue of stock. Sue, who is interested, has been studying the prospectus.*

protocol (PRO-to-kol): A program that allows one computer device to interact with another.

> *The technician explained that my printer is not working because my computer does not have the proper protocol to allow the printer to read from my computer.*

proviso (pro-VI-zo): A qualification or a condition.

> *Employees of Widgets Inc. get five weeks of vacation with the proviso that not all five can be taken at once.*

proxy (PROX-e): A person who has authorization to vote on behalf of a stockholder of a corporation.

> *Brett sent a proxy to the stockholders meeting.*

proxy statement (PROX-e STATE-ment): A report that the Securities and Exchange Commission requires be sent to shareholders who are going to vote by proxy on company matters.

Brett spent the afternoon studying the proxy statement from Widgets Inc.

psychic income (SI-kik IN-kum): Something besides money that one earns from a job.

The pay at Widgets Inc. wasn't good, but Stan derived a lot of psychic income from proudly telling people that he was a master widget maker.

public domain (PUB-lik do-MANE): Widely available information that is not copyrighted.

The Declaration of Independence is in the public domain. Anyone can publish it without asking permission.

publicly held corporation (PUB-lik-le held kor-po-RA-shun): A corporation that has common stock listed on a national stock exchange.

Widgets Inc. is a publicly held corporation. Its stock is traded on the New York Stock Exchange.

public offering (PUB-lik OFF-er-ing): Asking the public to buy stock. The act of going public.

Stuff Company is going public. The public offering is next week.

public record (PUB-lik REK-erd): Documents that must be legally recorded and available to the public.

The deed on that land is a matter of public record. Just go to the registrar of deeds.

public relations (PUB-lik re-LA-shuns): Communication about a company or product that is designed to improve its image. Often, public relations is used to pitch a story about a product or business to the media.

> *Widgets Inc. has launched a massive public relations campaign about its new high-tech widget.*

puffing (PUFF-ing): Exaggerating the qualities of a product to a customer.

> *The salesperson in the store was really puffing the new high-tech widget by Widgets Inc. He even said the high-tech widget has been proven to increase sex appeal.*

punitive damages (PU-nih-tiv DAM-ej-es): Legal compensation that is ordered in excess of actual damages suffered. Punitive damages are meant as a form of punishment.

> *The court ruled that Widgets Inc. deliberately put a dangerous widget on the market and ordered the company to pay $4 million in punitive damages to a consumer group. Widgets Inc. is appealing the decision.*

push incentives (push in-SEN-tivs): Money offered to retail salespersons to push a particular item.

> *Widgets Inc. has allocated a budget specifically for push incentives, in order to get the word about its high-tech widgets on the retail floor.*

put option (put OP-chun): An option to sell a specific number of shares of a stock at a set price by a certain date.

> *Howard has a put option on his Widgets Inc. stock. Even if the price goes down between now and the deadline of the put option, Howard has locked in a set price.*

pyramiding (PEER-ah-mid-ing): Use of profits from an investment to purchase other investments.

Alfred is pyramiding his profits from Widgets Inc. stock in order to buy stock in Stuff Company.

qualified stock option (KWAL-ih-fide stok OP-chun): Employee stock option that sets a low price for stock and freezes that price so that an employee can buy the stock later on at the same price.

Melinda loved being a top executive at Widgets Inc., and she especially loved the qualified stock option because Widgets Inc. stock always rose in price.

quality (KWAL-ih-te): A tough-to-measure indication of excellence and character.

We make quality widgets.

quality control (KWAL-ih-te kun-TROLE): Method of maintaining quality by systematically inspecting the product at various stages in the manufacturing process.

Widgets Inc. has built its reputation on its quality products, so of course it has a stringent program of quality control.

quarter (KWAR-ter): One-fourth of a year, it usually refers to one-fourth of a fiscal year.

Mark's boss told Mark that his department had its highest sales for a quarter in the history of the company, and that Mark was getting a big bonus.

quarterly report (KWAR-ter-le re-PORT): Financial report that is issued every three months, except when the annual report is issued. It is an unaudited summary of financial activity within a company.

Lisa was waiting to get the quarterly report before deciding whether to sell her Widgets Inc. stock.

quasi contract (KWAH-ze KON-trakt): A legal contract that is created by from the use of applying logic to a situation.

> *After a virus damaged his computer, Tony took it to a repair shop. Tony had his computer repaired, and it turned out that it also needed a new software program to fight against any future damage from the virus. Even though Tony didn't specifically contract for the software, he had a quasi contract to pay for it because the software itself made it possible for the repaired computer to function properly.*

quid pro quo (kwid pro kwo): Something in return for another thing.

> *The consultant smiled and said, "Quid pro quo. My time for your money."*

quota (KWO-tah): A predetermined, proportional number.

> *Widgets Inc. has a quota for the percentage of hires each month that must be an underrepresented minority.*

quotation (kwo-TA-shun): The declared price of something.

> *When I asked my broker how much stock from Widgets Inc. cost, I couldn't believe the high quotation.*

rally (RAL-le): An increase in the price of a security after a period of stagnation or dropping prices.

> *Widgets Inc. stock has had a rally in the past week.*

random access memory (RAM) (ram): The main memory of a computer. Every area of RAM can be accessed with equal ease.

> *My new computer came with sixteen megabytes of RAM.*

random sample (RAN-dum SAM-pl): When every member of a population has an equal chance of being picked, the ones that are selected are a random sample.

> *According to a survey of a random sample of widget consumers, the best thing about widgets is the fact that they are purple.*

rank and file (rank and file): Union members who vote but are not officers.

> *The union officials may have agreed to a contract, but nothing is firm until the rank and file votes.*

rapport (rah-POR): Getting along. A harmonious relationship achieved by effort.

> *Widgets Inc. has good rapport with its suppliers because it always makes huge orders and pays on time.*

rate of return (rate of re-TURN): A percentage earned from stock in a year as calculated by dividing the dividends earned by the price paid for the stock.

> *The rate of return on Widgets Inc. stock is 15 percent.*

ratio analysis (RA-she-o ah-NAL-ih-sis): A comparison of figures in financial statements for the purpose of making decisions about loans and investments. Ratios are used when comparing accounting periods or comparing companies.

> *My broker gave me a ratio analysis of Widgets Inc. and after reading it I want to invest even more money in the company.*

raw materials (raw mah-TEH-re-els): All of the elements that go into the manufacturing of a product.

> *The raw materials for widgets are purple plastic, metal screws, and rubber bands.*

read-only memory (ROM) (rom): The memory of a computer that does not need to be changed.

The ROM includes all the instructions that were written into the computer when it was manufactured.

real estate (RE-el es-TATE): Land and what is on and in it.

When Jed bought that piece of real estate, he had no idea that there was oil underground.

real income (RE-el IN-kum): The change in income of an individual as compared to change in overall consumer prices.

If your pay doesn't go up as much as prices, then your real income is actually going down.

real time (RE-el time): Time that occurs away from cyberspace.

Jane told her friends in the chat room, "I have to go, I have a real-time interruption."

realtor (RE-el-ter): A real estate broker who is a member of the local board and the National Association of Realtors.

Dexter went to see a realtor about putting his house on the market.

rebate (RE-bate): A refund.

John had a good day. First he received his tax rebate in the mail. Then he went to the store where he had recently bought a television and showed the manager an advertisement for the same television at a cheaper price. He received a rebate from the store.

reboot (re-BOOT): To electronically start up a computer all over again after it has already been running.

When my screen froze and I couldn't figure out how to get it to unfreeze, I decided to reboot my computer and start over.

recapitalization (re-KAP-ih-tel-ize-A-shun): A change in the capital structure of a corporation that is frequently done after bankruptcy.

Stuff Company is undergoing recapitalization by exchanging bonds for stock.

receivables (re-SEVE-ah-bls): List of claims held against customers for money, goods, or services.

Our receivables are really high right now.

receiver (re-SEVE-er): A person appointed by a court to take control of an entity that is in the midst of a form of bankruptcy called receivership.

A receiver is in charge of an entity until a disposition is made in court.

receivership (re-SEVE-er-ship): A form of bankruptcy in which a business is placed under the control of a receiver while an equitable remedy is worked out.

The Stuff family has lost control of Stuff Company, which has gone into a receivership.

recession (re-SESH-un): Two straight quarters of decline of the country's gross domestic product. A recession is a slowing of the economy.

The president is worried about a recession starting six months before the election.

reciprocity (res-ih-PROSS-ih-te): Mutual extending of privileges between two countries, companies, or people.

The U.S. is trying to get reciprocity with its trading partners concerning ease of access into each other's markets.

redlining (RED-line-ing): Illegally refusing to grant loans in certain neighborhoods.

> *Whitebread Bank has been charged with redlining because it refused to give loans in one part of the city.*

red tape (red tape): Bureaucratic paperwork that must be completed by several people before approval for something is granted.

> *Even though we are ready to start right now, I bet we don't start this project for a year because of all the red tape.*

re-engineering (RE-en-jih-NEER-ING): Process of re-examining how everything is done in an organization. Re-engineering starts at the beginning and redesigns everything all over again.

> *Many believe re-engineering is essential to keeping a company competitive, but others believe it is an excuse to lay people off.*

refinance (RE-fi-NANS): Refunding an existing debt, usually at a lower interest rate.

> *Greg is going to refinance his mortgage because interest rates have come down.*

refund check (re-FUND chek): Check to a taxpayer from the IRS when the taxpayer's withholding or estimated payments exceeded the tax for the year.

> *Vera is counting on her refund check to pay for her spring vacation to Florida.*

regional office (RE-jun-el OFF-fis): A branch office of a company that is responsible for company activities, often sales, in a particular region.

> *Widgets Inc. sent the complaint that came from Ohio to its regional office in Cleveland.*

registrar (REJ-is-trar): A person who is responsible for keeping accurate records.

Joseph went to see the registrar of deeds to check the record of the land he may buy.

regressive tax (re-GRES-siv tax): A tax in which poor people pay a higher percentage of their earnings than rich people do.

A 5 percent tax on food is regressive because both rich and poor people pay the same amount, but that amount is a larger percentage of a poor person's income.

regulated industry (REG-u-late-ed IN-dus-tre): An industry that is regulated by government.

Although the pricing of the airline industry has been deregulated, it is a regulated industry with regard to safety concerns.

regulations (reg-u-LA-shuns): Rules that must be followed to operate in an industry.

Widgets Inc. didn't like all the new regulations in the widget industry, but it hired a bunch of lawyers to make sure it was following the new rules.

regulatory agency (REG-u-lah-toh-re A-jen-se): An agency charged with ensuring regulations are followed. A regulatory agency makes rulings and can issue sanctions.

The Department of Public Utilities is the regulatory agency that sets utility rates.

reinstatement (re-in-STATE-ment): Restoration of insurance.

As soon as Beth paid her overdue bill, she was eligible for reinstatement.

remote host (re-MOTE hoste): The computer that your computer (the local host) connects to in a Telnet connection.

The remote host is on the other side of the country.

renewal (re-NEW-el): Restoration of an insurance policy, which usually happens automatically when a premium is paid.

There will be renewal of your policy as soon as you pay your overdue premium.

reorder point (re-OR-der point): Point of inventory depletion at which a reorder is supposed to occur.

The reorder point for widgets in our store is when we are down to 100 widgets.

reorganization (re-OR-gen-i-ZA-shun): A change in the financial structure of a business. This frequently occurs when a company files for Chapter 11 bankruptcy.

Stuff Company is undergoing a reorganization.

repetitive manufacturing (re-PET-ih-tiv man-u-FAK-chure-ing): A process of making large quantities of an item by doing the same steps over and over.

Widgets, just like automobiles and candy bars, are made by repetitive manufacturing.

replacement cost (re-PLASE-ment kost): Insurance term for how much it would cost to make or replace of an item that is now owned.

After the fire, the insurance company did a study of the replacement cost of that building.

reporting currency (re-PORT-ing KUR-ren-se): The currency that a company uses in its financial reports.

The reporting currency for Widgets Inc. is the American dollar.

request for proposals (RFP) (re-KWEST for pro-POZE-els): Announcement that bids will be accepted for a specific project.

A request for proposals went out for a company to manage the city's train stations.

research & development (R&D) (r and d): The process of logically developing a product by figuring out what can be made, and then finding a market that needs it. Both the scientific and marketing research have bearing on the exact form of the final product.

The R&D department did an incredible job of designing and marketing the high-tech widget.

research intensive (re-SEARCH in-TEN-siv): A project that requires many man-hours of research.

This report has been research intensive.

resident buyer (REZ-ih-dent BI-er): An individual who has an office in a specific merchandising area and keeps a company informed about the market.

Molly is the Widgets Inc. resident buyer in Denver. She keeps an eye on the widget departments of many Denver stores.

resolution (rez-o-LU-shun): The clarity of a computer screen.

My new monitor has high resolution.

resources (re-SOURCEs): Everything needed to run an organization, including money, people, time, equipment, and raw materials.

Carol must decide how to allocate resources in her small startup company.

responsibility center (re-spon-sih-bil-ih-te SEN-ter): The part of an organization that controls investments, costs, or revenues.

The group in charge of investments is the investment center, which is the responsibility center for investments.

restructuring (re-STRUK-chure-ing): Reorganizing a company in a broad way that could include the way a company is financed or the way in which operations run.

> *Widgets Inc. is undergoing a restructuring. When it is finished, many people will probably lose their jobs.*

resume (REH-zu-ma): A document that shows one's education and work history. It is given to a potential employer.

> *After Jenny was laid off from Widgets Inc., she put together a new resume and started looking for a new job.*

retail (RE-tale): The business of selling to the public.

> *Ronald is opening a retail store selling widgets exclusively.*

retained earnings (re-TANED ERN-ings): Net profits that a business keeps after dividends are paid.

> *Widgets Inc. needs its retained earnings to build, so it can think about expanding into Europe.*

retainer (re-TANE-er): A fee paid up front to a professional for services expected to be performed.

> *The lawyer asked Widgets Inc. for a $10,000 retainer.*

retirement income (re-TIRE-ment IN-kum): The money a retired person regularly receives.

> *Social Security is my grandpa's only retirement income.*

retroactive (ret-ro-AKT-iv): A policy that, once enacted, takes effect from a prior time.

> *Widgets Inc. granted everyone in the company a pay raise retroactive to January 1.*

return on equity (re-TURN on EK-wih-te): A percentage earned on an investment. It is figured by taking the amount earned for a given time period and dividing it by the amount invested.

Dale received a 10 percent return on equity for his investment in Widgets Inc. stock.

returns (re-TURNS): Merchandise that is returned to a supplier. Credit is given for return.

Every month, the president of Widgets Inc. is very concerned about returns.

revenue (REV-eh-nu): The gross amount earned.

Widgets Inc. has a new high-tech widget out, and sales of the product have almost doubled the revenues of the company.

reversal (re-VER-sel): A change in the direction of a security.

The stock of Widgets Inc., which was plummeting, has undergone a reversal since the introduction of the high-tech widget.

reverse discrimination (re-VERS dis-krim-ih-NA-shun): Illegally favoring minorities and women for job placement at the expense of others who may be more qualified.

If hiring quotas are put into place without a proper affirmative action plan, there could be reverse discrimination.

rider (RI-der): A clause or provision in an insurance policy that changes some aspect of coverage, either by adding coverage or excluding coverage.

There is a rider on my policy for a higher deductible than normal.

right of first refusal (rite of first re-FUZE-el): Opportunity given to match the terms of a contract before the contract is completed.

Arthur was offered a job from Stuff Company but his current employer, which had a right of first refusal with Arthur, matched the offer and kept Arthur as a Widgets employee.

right-to-work law (rite to werk law): A law in some states that outlaws the requirement that someone belong to a union before he can work in a particular shop.

Because of the right-to-work laws down South, many northern companies have relocated so they can avoid labor problems.

risk (risk): Condition in which there is more than one posssible outcome, and the outcome can be good or bad. If you know how much of a risk something is, you know the probability of a good outcome instead of a bad one.

With any new venture, there is always some risk.

risk avoidance (risk ah-VOID-ens): Method of management to avoid risk.

Widgets Inc. is very comfortable at the top of the market and is now engaged in a strategy of risk avoidance.

role playing (role PLA-ing): A training exercise in which participants simulate a situation by taking on roles.

The sales manager loved to use role playing to teach her salespeople sales techniques.

roll over (role O-ver): Putting one debt in place of another.

We are going to roll over the mortgage for one with a lower interest rate.

royalty (ROY-el-te): The percentage of profit that is paid to a creative person, such as an author, or to the owner of a property that is being exploited by another, such as a piece of land that contains oil.

Stephen King doesn't need any more royalty checks, but he never turns them down.

sabotage (SAB-o-tazh): Deliberate destruction of or interference with a place of business.

Widgets Inc. is concerned about sabotage after it received a threatening phone call from someone who identified himself as an ex-employee.

sack (sak): To terminate someone's employment.

Joe is very depressed because he was sacked from his job today.

safekeeping (SAFE-KEEP-ing): Protecting assets in storage.

My grandmother gave me the original stock certificates from Widgets Inc. for safekeeping, so I put them in a safe-deposit box.

salary (SAL-ah-re): Compensation an employee receives for employment. A salary is a regular payment and is not dependent on hours worked, as is an hourly wage.

Ralph took a job with Widgets Inc. for a very large salary.

sale (sale): A trade of goods for money.

The clerk handed me the widget and I handed him the money. The sale was complete.

sales and leaseback (sales and LESE-bak): An arrangement where the owner of a property sells it to another party and then leases the same property from the new owner.

Stuff Company has a sales and leaseback arrangement with Widgets Inc. Stuff Company is selling its building to Widgets Inc. and then leasing it back from Widgets Inc.

sales budget (sales BUDJ-et): The amount of sales that is expected from a product, area, or salesperson within a given time period.

The salesman complained that the sales budget is so high that he will never live up to expectations.

sales office (sales OFF-fis): An office owned by a manufacturer that is used to promote sales in a geographic area.

I am going to pay a visit to the San Francisco sales office.

salesperson (sales PER-sun): One whose job it is to sell the product of a company.

Tim is the newest salesperson at Widgets Inc.

sales promotion (sales pro-MO-shun): Activities and techniques used to sell a product.

Widgets Inc. is running a sales promotion sweepstakes with lottery-like scratch cards.

sampling (SAM-pling): Questioning a small group of people about a product. The small group is meant to be representative of the desires of the population as a whole.

Widgets Inc. is sampling a group of customers at the local mall.

savings & loan association (S&L) (ess and el): An institution similar to a savings bank except that the primary purpose of an S&L is to give out loans for houses.

We have our mortgage through an S&L.

savings bank (SAVE-ings bank): A bank that concentrates its efforts on the savings account.

My savings account is in a savings bank.

savings bond (SAVE-ings bond): Federal bond in denominations from $50 to $10,000. These bonds are paid at face value when they reach maturity.

> *Stephanie always gives her grandchildren savings bonds on their birthdays.*

scabs (skabs): Nonunion workers brought in to do the work of striking union employees.

> *Jim believed in everything unions stood for but he needed money, so he crossed the picket line despite his beliefs, and he went to work as a scab.*

scale (skale): The rate of wages for those performing a specific job.

> *The union scale for a first-year widget maker is $15 per hour.*

scatter plan (SKAT-ter plan): An advertising plan for broadcast media in which advertisements are aired at a variety of times on different stations and on different programs.

> *Last year, Widgets Inc. sponsored the soap opera, Moments of Passion, but this year the company is trying to reach a broader audience with a scatter plan.*

scheduled production (SKED-uled pro-DUK-shun): Timetable for a production sequence.

> *The scheduled production for your order of widgets is next week.*

sealed bid (seled bid): An estimate of the cost of a project that a company or person wants to do. A sealed bid is kept private from competitors.

> *Widgets Inc. submitted a sealed bid to the state of Montana for the widget contract in the Montana schools.*

seasonal business (SE-zun-el BIZ-ness): A business that only flourishes during part of the year.

> *A ski resort is a seasonal business, and so is a snack bar on a beach in Maine.*

seasonal employment/unemployment (SE-zun-el em-PLOY-ment/un-em-PLOY-ment): Employment, or unemployment, that is expected at certain times of the year.

> *On Cape Cod, seasonal employment is highest in the summer, and seasonal unemployment is highest in the winter.*

seat (sete): Membership on a securities exchange.

> *John told me that if you have a seat on the New York Stock Exchange, you are a player.*

secondary boycott (SEK-und-ahr-e): A union boycott of a company that is doing business with a company the union is fighting.

> *The Widgetmakers union did a secondary boycott of Bigstore Company in hopes of forcing that store to quit buying widgets from the nonunion Stuff Company.*

Section 8 Housing (SEK-chun ate HOUS-ing): Private dwelling units rented out to low-income tenants under the Section 8 program of the 1937 Housing Act. Under the program, landlords receive a portion of the rent due from the government, and the rest from the low-income tenant.

> *The Joneses bought a new house and rented their old one out through Section 8 Housing.*

sector (SEK-ter): Stocks from one industry.

> *There are a few analysts who follow the widget sector of the market.*

secured bond (seh-KURED bond): A bond that is backed by some form of collateral.

My father-in-law advised me to invest in secured bonds.

secured debt (seh-KURED det): Debt, including bonds, that is backed by some form of security.

The loan James took out to start his business is a secured debt. He put his house up as collateral.

securities (seh-KU-rih-tees): Stocks and bonds.

Jimmy can't wait to graduate from college and start making some money so that he can invest in securities. He has decided he will get rich investing in securities.

Securities and Exchange Commission (SEC) (seh-KU-rih-tees and ex-CHANJE KUM-mish-un): Federal agency that oversees the investment industry and keeps a close eye out for unfair practices, and ensures that investors are properly informed.

The SEC has a close eye on the merger of Widgets Inc. and Stuff Company.

seed money (seed MUN-e): The initial money given by a venture capitalist to a startup firm.

Vivian, who always dreamed of owning a widget company, took the seed money and rented a building and bought a used widget press. It was the happiest moment of her life.

segmentation strategy (seg-men-TA-shun STRAT-eh-je): A strategy of marketing in which the focus of effort is one specific segment of the market.

Widgets Inc. has a segmentation strategy of focusing on southern males.

self-employed (self em-PLOYD): A person who works for himself. Such a person is responsible for everything produced, and must pay a self-employment tax that takes the place of Social Security payments.

>*Kevin is a freelance writer who sells his articles to many different magazines. He is a self-employed worker.*

seller financing (SEL-er fi-NANS-ing): Financing of the purchase of a property by a seller. This can be used as an inducement to buy.

>*When Steve bought his parent's house, it was with seller financing.*

seller's market (SEL-ers MAR-ket): Market in which there is more demand than supply. In such a market, prices tend to go up.

>*The real estate market in this resort town is a seller's market because so many people from the city want to move here.*

selling short (SEL-ing short): Strategy of making money by borrowing stock from a broker, selling it, and hoping it drops in price so you can buy it back at a lower price and return it to the broker, thus making a profit.

>*Jonathan is hoping the price of Widgets Inc. drops so he can buy back the stock he borrowed and sold. He is always trying to make a profit by selling short.*

semiconductors (SEM-i-kun-DUKT-ers): Substances such as silicon that have variable conductivity depending on temperature. Semiconductors are an essential part of a computer.

>*Widgets Inc. put semiconductors in its high-tech widget.*

seminar (SEM-ih-nar): A course for people who come together to study or research a particular subject.

>*Ethel is attending the widgetmaker's high-tech seminar in Las Vegas.*

serial bond (SE-re-el bond): A bond that does not mature all at once but instead matures with a number of payments or installments.

Arnold bought his daughter a serial bond that will mature once a year when she is in college.

serial port (SE-re-el port): A port on a computer into which you can plug things such as a mouse, a modem, a CD-ROM, a printer, or other peripherals.

You have to find the right serial port to plug in your printer.

server (SERV-er): Computer that runs a network of computers.

James had a hard time getting on the Internet because the server he usually uses was not responding.

service (SERV-is): Something that one person or company does for another.

A consultant sells a service, as does a limousine company.

service economy (SERV-is e-KON-o-me): An economy that is more dependent upon service business than it is on manufacturing.

Any resort town is inevitably a service economy.

service jobs/workers (SERV-is jobs): Jobs or people who have jobs that are set up to provide services for others rather than to make things.

Karl complained that the only jobs around here are low-paying service jobs. He said he wants to move somewhere to get a manufacturing job.

settlement (SET-tl-ment): A negotiated agreement.

Widgets Inc. and the union have reached a settlement on the contract.

severance pay (SEV-er-ens pay): Pay that is given to an employee who has been terminated.

Widgets Inc. gave Grant $2,000 in severance pay.

sexual harassment (SEX-u-el HA-rass-ment): Illegal discrimination against an employee because an employee declines sexual advances. The harassment can be the advances themselves or the job discrimination against the employee who turned down the advances.

Edgar Widget has been charged with sexual harassment by his secretary, who says he made sexual comments to her every day for thirty-five years.

shakedown (SHAKE-down): A test run of a product to try to catch any last-second glitches.

Widgets Inc. sent out its high-tech widget for free to a group of 100 people as a sort of shakedown before it goes to market.

share (shar): When a company goes public and issues stock, a share is one piece equal to all other shares of the ownership of the company.

For my graduation present, my grandfather gave me 1,000 shares of stock in Widgets Inc.

shared appreciation mortgage (shaird ap-pre-she-A-shun MOR-gej): A loan for a residential property with below-market interest rates. The lender is given some percentage of the appreciation of the property over a specified time period.

Donna has a shared appreciation mortgage. She hated to give away some of the appreciation in her house, but it was the only mortgage she could get.

shared equity mortgage (shaird EK-wih-te MOR-gej): A residential loan that grants the lender a portion of the equity in the home. When the house is sold, the buyer and lender split the equity.

> *Larry sold his house but he didn't get as big of a profit as it would be expected because he had a shared equity mortgage and had to share the equity with his lender.*

shareholder (SHAIR-HOLD-er): Someone who owns stock in a company.

> *For Sam's graduation, his father bought him some stock in Widgets Inc. Ever since he became a shareholder, he doesn't go a day without reading the* Wall Street Journal.

shareware (SHAIR-wair): Software that is distributed by modem on the honor system. People can download shareware and try it for free. If they like it, they are supposed to send a payment to the people who developed it.

> *Joe downloaded some accounting shareware for his new company, but he didn't like it so he is not going to pay the fee.*

shell corporation (shell kor-po-RA-shun): Incorporated company that doesn't do anything. Such a corporation is set up to get financing to start operations. Or . . . A corporation set up to hide illegal activities.

> *Aaron set up a shell corporation before he started going after financing for his new widget business. Or . . . Zola Inc. is a shell corporation set up by a group of red-eyed drug dealers trying to hide their profits.*

shop (shop): A place of work where things are produced.

> *Kevin just received a job in the widget shop on the other side of town.*

short bond (short bond): A bond that matures in less than a year.

> *Widgets Inc. issued a number of short bonds to pay for its new factory.*

shortfall (SHORT-fall): Less than was expected.

Widgets Inc. is experiencing a revenue shortfall because of so many problems with the much-hyped high-tech widget.

shrinkage (SHRINGK-kej): The difference between what the amount of inventory is by a count versus how much should there be according to the book.

The president of Widgets Inc. is convinced the company is overrun with employee theft because of the high rate of shrinkage of inventory.

shutdown (SHUT-DOWN): When production stops for any number of reasons, including breakdown of equipment or lack of workers.

The union is threatening a shutdown of Widgets Inc. if negotiations on a new contract don't make progress.

sick pay (sik pa): Pay that is given to a worker who is sick.

One of the bad parts about being self-employed is that there is no sick pay. If you don't work, you don't get paid.

silent partner (SI-lent PART-ner): A limited partner. A silent partner has no role in the management of the company and is only liable for the amount he/she invested.

Juanita is a silent partner in Widgets Inc.

signing bonus (SINE-ing BO-nus): The up-front money given to a sports star who signs a contract with a professional team.

Joe Jumper received an $8 million signing bonus with the Boston Celtics in addition to his ten-year, $99 million contract. Joe said, "I'm going to give it all to charity." Then he laughed.

Silicon Valley (SIL-ih-kon VAL-le): Area in northern California that is a center of high-tech business and research.

Adam graduated from MIT and took a job in Silicon Valley.

simulation (sim-u-LA-shun): Using a computer mathematical model to represent a real situation.

> *Widgets Inc. did a simulation of the widget market to prove that its high-tech widget would sell.*

skill obsolescence (skill ob-so-LES-ens): When an occupational skill is no longer of any use to a business because technology can do the job better and quicker.

> *Fifty years ago, Arnold the widget carver faced skill obsolescence because of the new widget press. Now, Arnold's grandson Andy faces skill obsolescence because of technology that allows the widget press to run without human assistance.*

sleeper (SLEEP-er): A stock that few know of but that has a great chance of growing in price.

> *William was happy to have recognized that Stuff Company was a sleeper stock. The price shot way up after he bought it and now he is living in a mansion on the ocean.*

slander (SLAN-der): Words intended to damage another's reputation.

> *After the president of Stuff Company called the president of Widgets Inc. "a deliberate polluter and a liar," the president of Widgets Inc. sued for slander.*

slogan (SLO-gen): A catchy phrase used to sell a product or a company.

> *Executives at Widgets Inc. were split about whether they liked the new company slogan, "Widgets for a Wobbly World."*

slowdown (SLO-down): A deliberate slowing of production by union workers to try to force a company to negotiate.

> *The union members said they could not afford a strike so they decided to try a slowdown to force the company's hand.*

slush fund (slush fund): An account that has extra money in it that is used to administer bribes.

> *Richard Nixon's cronies had a slush fund set up to get people to be quiet about Watergate.*

Small Business Administration (SBA) (small BIZ-ness ad-min-is-TRA-shun): A federal agency set up to help small businesses with information and loans.

> *Roger received a low-interest loan from the SBA so he could rent an office for his widget repair business.*

small investor (small in-VEST-er): A low-budget investor who buys small amounts of stock.

> *"This company owes the thousands of small investors who believed in us," said the founder of the company.*

snowballing (SNO-ball-ing): A business activity that quickly gains momentum.

> *We started advertising the high-tech widgets, and the market has been snowballing ever since.*

soft spot (soft spot): A small weakness in an otherwise robust company, activity, or type of stock.

> *Although Widgets Inc. puts out a great product at a fair price with decent marketing, the one soft spot of the company is its service department.*

software (SOFT-wair): The programs that operate a computer.

> *I have new word processing software that allows me to do news releases, newsletters, or a 300-page novel manuscript.*

sole proprietorship (sole pro-PRI-eh-tur-ship): A business owned and run by one person.

> *Joe's Widgets is a sole proprietorship.*

solvency (SOL-ven-se): The ability to pay bills that are due.

Finally, at thirty-five, Rich reached the point of solvency.

solvent (SOL-vent): The state a company is in when it can pay bills as they come due.

Stuff Company is solvent. It always pays its bills on time.

special interest group (IN-ter-est group): A group, often political, that has a common concern and goal.

The Widget Protection Society is a special interest group lobbying Congress to declare antique widgets to be national treasures.

special purchase (SPESH-el PUR-ches): A term for lower-cost, lower-quality merchandise. When something is advertised as a special purchase, the low cost is highlighted.

Widgets Inc. always had to compete with the widgets from other companies that were put up as a special purchase by retailers.

specialty advertising (SPESH-el-te AD-ver-tize-ing): Advertising that uses a medium other than traditional print and broadcast. Such advertising includes bumper stickers, buttons, and coffee mugs.

Congressman Neon Sign said his favorite part of running for office is dreaming up new forms of specialty advertising.

specifications (spe-sih-fih-KA-shuns): Detailed directions or detailed list given with a product or purchase order.

The electrician working on the new house noticed that the specifications call for five outlets in every room.

speculate (SPEK-u-late): Investing in a risky proposition in the hopes of making lots of quick money.

> *Eighty-nine years ago, my great-grandfather speculated his entire savings in a small company called Widgets Inc., which is now the world's largest producer of widgets. I have a picture of my great-grandfather in each of my nine mansions.*

speculative building (SPEK-u-lah-tiv BIL-ding): Constructing a building or house with the expectation that it will sell when it is completed.

> *Jason is developing a street with twenty houses. Three are being custom built. The rest have not sold. Jason is doing some speculative building of four houses to try and sell them.*

spillover (SPILL-O-ver): An effect a business has on those not involved in the business, such as neighbors.

> *The Widgets Inc. factory had a positive spillover effect on all the local taverns, especially every Friday.*

spin-off (spin off): When one company splits away from another and the shareholders of the first are automatically granted shares in the new company.

> Widgetworld *magazine is a spin-off of Widgets Inc.*

splintered authority (SPLIN-terd aw-THOR-ih-te): When many managers have some degree of authority over a decision.

> *There is so much splintered authority at Widgets Inc. that it takes five managers just to approve a $50 travel voucher.*

spirit (SPIR-it): The animating principle of an organization.

> *Everyone in Widgets Inc. is so depressed. There is not much spirit there.*

spokesperson (SPOKES-PER-sun): A person who speaks for the company or product. A spokesperson may be a celebrity, or an employee of the company.

> *Basketball superstar Joe Jumper said, "I like my widgets from Widgets Inc. because Widgets Inc. makes wonderful widgets." Jumper was paid $5 million to be a Widgets Inc. spokesperson. His entire duties were to utter that sentence.*

sponsor (SPON-ser): An advertiser who buys air time on a television program or who supports some event such as a tennis match or the Olympics.

> *Widgets Inc. is an official sponsor of the Widgets 500 race in Toledo.*

spread (spred): The difference between the high price and low price of a stock during a specific period.

> *The price of Widgets Inc. stock stayed steady all of last year. There is only a small spread for last year.*

spreadsheet (SPRED-sheet): A table of numbers in rows and columns that is used for accounting purposes.

> *Widgets Inc. just bought the newest accounting software from Smartypants Software. It includes an easy-to-use spreadsheet.*

squeeze (skweze): Situation in which costs are rising and money is harder to come by.

> *Stuff Company is undergoing a squeeze that came from trying to compete with the much larger Widgets Inc.*

staff (staff): The people who work for a company.

> *The boss always asks the staff where they want to have the company Christmas party.*

staggering maturities (STAG-ger-ing mah-CHURE-ih-tes): A investment strategy of buying short-, medium-, and long-term bonds to hedge against interest rates.

Sue is staggering maturities because she is a cautious investor.

stand-alone system (stand ah-LONE SIS-tem): A work station that one person uses and is not connected to anything else.

My personal computer was a stand-alone system until I connected to the Internet.

Standard & Poor's Rating (STAND-erd and poors RATE-ing): A classification of the riskiness of a stock or bond. The top grades are: AAA, AA, A, and BBB.

My broker recommends having at least half of my money in a security with a Standard & Poor's Rating of at least AA.

standard deduction (STAND-erd de-DUK-shun): Deduction the government gives to a taxpayer who chooses not to itemize deductions.

Ron figured his own taxes but he forgot the basic standard deduction. Next year, Ron is going to an accountant.

standard deviation (STAND-erd de-ve-A-SHUN): A statistic that measures the tendency of an individual value to vary from the mean.

There is a a low standard deviation to the price of Widgets Inc. stock. This means the stock is not risky.

standard of living (STAND-erd of LIV-ing): The way a consumer lives, taking into account all possessions and goods that are used and consumed.

"Look around," she said sarcastically. "Our standard of living is not exactly the same as that guy who owns that computer company."

startup (START-up): A new business.

When Stuff Company was a startup, it found some naive venture capitalists to believe that it could compete with mighty Widgets Inc.

startup costs (START-up kosts): The costs of a new business in the stage between when the decision to start a business is made and when the business actually starts operations.

The startup costs in the widget industry are very high because the widget equipment is so darn expensive.

statistical sampling (stah-TIS-tik-el SAM-pling): A sample taken from the whole to give a reading on how the whole group stands.

We did a statistical sampling of our customers and found that a great majority of them want a choice of blue or red widgets.

status symbol (STAH-tus SIM-bul): Some possession that costs lots of money that is representative of the individual's wealth and taste.

Edgar Widget, the president of Widgets Inc., kept ponies on his estate as a status symbol.

statute of limitations (STACH-ute of lim-ih-TA-shuns): The length of time that a person, or the state, is given to make a legal claim.

Arthur was still worried about his tax return from three decades ago, even though the statute of limitations for the IRS to investigate ran out years ago.

staying power (STA-ing POW-er): The ability to stick with an investment in bad times.

Edgar Widget, the president of Widgets Inc., has staying power to last through the recession, no matter how long it lasts.

steward (STEW-erd): A union official who takes care of day-to-day union business in a union shop.

Tom is a union steward at Widgets Inc.

stipend (STI-pend): Payment for services.

> *Alice received a generous stipend from Widgets Inc. for that project.*

stock (stok): A portion of ownership in a corporation.

> *Judy owns stock in Widgets Inc.*

stockholder (STOK-HOLDE-er): A person who owns stock in a corporation.

> *Judy is a stockholder in Widgets Inc.*

stock option (stok OP-chun): Employee compensation program, especially for executives. It allows employees to purchase stock at a set price, either at or below market value, for a set period of time.

> *Judy likes working at Widgets Inc. because the stock option is such a good program.*

stop payment (stop PAY-ment): Canceling payment of a check that has not yet been cashed.

> *The check that Widgets Inc. sent to Mary the consultant was lost in the mail. The company ordered a stop payment on that check and it sent her another one.*

store brand (stor brand): A product that carries the name of the retail store that sells it.

> *For some reason, Teresa likes store-brand coffee better than the coffee sold by the big companies.*

straight-line method of depreciation (strate line METH-ud of de-pre-she-A-shun): Depreciation method in which an equal amount of an asset's value is written off each year for the useful life of the product.

> *Widgets Inc. did a straight-line depreciation of its new widget press.*

straight time (strate time): Work for a regular hourly wage. Not overtime.

Widgets Inc. wants to pay its employees straight time for working on Christmas.

street smarts (street smarts): Knowledge that one has from life rather than from formal education.

Ralph didn't even graduate from high school but the boss likes him because he has street smarts.

strike (strike): When employees refuse to work as a means of putting pressure on the employer.

When the union at Widgets Inc. could not get the company to talk about even a small pay raise, it decided to try a strike against the company.

strike pay (strike pa): Pay given to union members from a union during a work stoppage. The money comes from funds collected while workers are working.

Quentin believed in the union and the strike, but if it wasn't for the strike pay, he wouldn't be able to feed his family.

strike vote (strike vote): The formal vote by union members on whether to go on strike.

Tom knew that a good part of his future was tied up in tomorrow's strike vote.

structural inflation (STRUK-chure-el in-FLA-shun): The inflation that is an integral part of an economic system.

You cannot stop inflation completely. In the U.S. economic system, there is some degree of structural inflation.

subliminal advertising (sub-lim-ih-nel AD-ver-tize-ing): Advertising that is not obvious but rather is presented to the subconscious. One way is to put a very brief image of a product into a movie and show that brief image several times a minute. Such advertising was ruled illegal in the 1950s.

> *When Ron was a child he used to go watch cowboy movies at the theater, and he always became thirsty for a certain brand of soda. It wasn't until years later that Ron figured he was probably subjected to subliminal advertising in that theater.*

subsidiary (sub-SID-e-air-e): A corporation that is run and owned by another corporation.

> *Stuff Company is a subsidiary of Widgets Inc.*

subsistence (sub-SIST-ens): A standard of living in which a person earns enough for the basics of life like food and shelter, but nothing more.

> *The union complained that Widgets Inc. barely pays subsistence wages.*

sunshine law (SUN-shine law): A law requiring the meetings of regulatory government bodies to be held in a public setting.

> *The sunshine law requires that all meetings of the Widget Regulatory Agency to be held in public.*

supercomputer (SU-per-kum-PUTE-er): Expensive, powerful computer used for complex scientific or mathematical problems.

> *The university has a new supercomputer for its engineering department.*

Super NOW Account (SU-per now uh-COUNT): A checking account that bears interest greater than a regular NOW account, but lower than a money market fund.

> *Josie put some of her Christmas bonus in a Super NOW Account.*

supply (SUP-pli): The amount of a commodity that is available to the market.

There is a good supply of widgets in the Phoenix market.

supply-side economics (SUP-pli side e-ko-NOM-iks): A theory of economics that says if taxes are cut, investors will use the money not paid in taxes to invest in and grow the economy.

There are politicians crossing the country preaching a sermon of supply-side economics.

surety bond (SHURE-te bond): A contract in which a third party backs the ability of another party to perform a specific task or pay a bill. The third party takes responsiblity for the contract if the person who signed the contract is unable to fulfill it.

My father signed a surety bond for me to start up a business.

surtax (SUR-tax): A tax on top of a tax.

The state put a 10 percent surtax on luxury items that has been hurting the yacht business.

sweatshop (SWET-shop): A workplace that has bad working conditions, poor wages, and long hours.

Johnny complained that working at Widgets Inc. is like working in a sweatshop.

swing shift (swing shift): The middle shift of a twenty-four-hour workday. It begins in midafternoon and ends at midnight.

Roger took the swing shift at Widgets Inc. so that he could also work during the day as a janitor at the local high school.

sympathetic strike (simp-ah-THET-ik strike): A strike that is not specifically against an employer but rather is a show of solidarity with a union involved in a current dispute.

The Widget Workers Union of America is striking against Stuff Company. It may do a sympathy strike against Stuff Company's parent company, Widgets Inc.

systems programmer (SIS-tems PRO-gram-er): The person who writes programs that allow a computer system to operate.

Fred took a job as systems programmer at Widgets Inc. because he wants the challenge of redesigning a production line system.

take a bath (take ah bath): To lose a bunch of money.

I should have never invested in Widgets Inc. Its high-tech widget turned out to be a dud. Then the stock plummeted and I took a bath.

takeover (TAKE-o-ver): A change in who owns and runs a company.

There is a rumor going around that Widgets Inc. is going to try to stage a takeover of Stuff Company.

tangible asset (TAN-jih-bl ASS-set): An asset that exists in the physical world.

Land is a tangible asset, and so is a chair.

target market (TAR-get MAR-ket): The people that a company wants to buy its products.

Widgets Inc. has a target market of southern males who own more than one gun.

tariff (TAR-iff): A federal tax on imports used to raise prices of imports in order to protect the local market for domestic companies.

Widgets Inc. was instrumental in getting Congress to vote for a higher tariff on imported widgets.

task force (task fors): A group of people temporarily assigned to work toward a specific objective.

> *Renee was assigned to the task force studying widget marketing to women.*

tax (tax): Money a citizen is responsible to pay. Tax money is used to run the government. Taxes can be on income, property, sales, or other areas.

> *There is a tax on widget sales, and a tax on my income.*

tax bracket (tax BRAK-et): Income level at which an individual or company must be in a certain tax rate. Different tax brackets pay different rates of taxes.

> *The only bad part about Joe getting a raise is that he is now in a higher tax bracket.*

tax credit (tax KRED-it): A straight reduction in taxes that a taxpayer must pay. This is different from a deduction in the amount of taxable income.

> *When Sue and Alex had a baby, they knew they would get a tax credit.*

tax-exempt security (tax ex-EMPT seh-KYU-rih-te): A bond that is exempt from taxes because it is offered by a city, state, or other government.

> *Joe has invested in municipal bonds because they are a tax-exempt security.*

tax incentives (tax in-SEN-tivs): The use of the tax system to encourage certain activities.

> *The state is offering tax incentives to large businesses to locate in the state.*

tax planning (tax PLAN-ing): The study of ways to reduce tax liability.

After Jane received her inheritance, her accountant recommended she do some tax planning.

team building (teme BILD-ing): Process of encouraging people to work together and giving them the motivation and the tools to work together.

Widgets Inc. is sending its top executives on a retreat dedicated to team building.

teamwork (TEME-werk): When a group of people work together toward a goal.

Widgets Inc. management commended the research and development department for its teamwork in making the high-tech widget a reality.

teaser ad (TEZE-er ad): A short advertisement that is designed to attract attention to an upcoming advertising campaign. A teaser ad does not identify the product, it merely makes the viewer curious to see the next advertisement.

Widgets Inc. ran a teaser advertisement before its campaign for the high-tech widget.

telecommunications (TEL-eh-kom-MU-nih-KA-shuns): Com-munication by radio, television, telephone, or telegraph.

Fred wants to invest in a telecommunications company.

telemarketing (TEL-eh-MAR-ket-ing): Selling over the telephone.

George works in the telemarketing department of Widgets Inc. He sold more widgets by phone last month than anyone else.

tender offer (TEN-der OFF-fer): An offer to buy stock from the shareholders of a corporation. The offer may only be valid if the offerer can get all the stock that it wants.

Harry is considering a tender offer for his Widgets Inc. stock.

testimonial (tes-tih-MO-ne-el): A statement from a credible source about the value of a product.

Joe Jumper, the basketball player, offered a testimonial on the back of the new basketball being sold by Bigsports Company.

test market (test MAR-ket): A geographic area that a company chooses in which to launch a new product or advertising campaign.

Widgets Inc. has always chosen Columbus, Ohio, as its test market.

thermal printer (THER-mel PRINT-er): Printer that works by using heat.

Ethel bought a thermal printer because it was inexpensive and quiet.

third party (thurd PART-e): A person or entity that does not have a direct interest in a deal.

Greg is a consultant to both Widgets Inc. and Stuff Company and is, in a sense, a third party to the merger.

three-martini lunch (three mar-TE-ne lunch): A symbol of excessive business write-offs.

Back in the 1980s, we used to go out for a three-martini lunch and write it off. But in 1993, Congress ruled that business people can only write off 50 percent of the cost of a business meal.

ticker (TICK-er): A running display of stock activity.

Val is always tuned to the business channel because he wants to keep a constant eye on the ticker.

tight money (tite MUN-e): When credit is hard to get.

> *Widgets Inc. is experiencing a tight money situation right now because banks are simply leery of lending money in these economic times.*

time management (time MAN-ej-ment): Figuring the best way to manage a daily schedule.

> *On Jim's performance evaluation, his boss wrote that Jim must do a better job of time management.*

title (TI-tl): Proof of ownership.

> *When I bought a used car, the title was transferred to me.*

title search (TI-tl surch): A study of public records regarding the history of a title to see if there are any liens affecting the property.

> *My attorney told me the next step toward buying the property would be a title search.*

toggle (TOG-gl): A key combination on a computer that turns something on, and then if pressed again it turns the same thing off.

> *On my keyboard, if I hit Caps Lock, it will lock in capital letters, and if I hit it again it will lock in lowercase letters. The Caps Lock key acts as a toggle switch.*

topping out (TOP-ing out): A security that is reaching its peak price and is expected to stabilize or decline.

> *Some experts say that the high-tech widget has run its course of successs and that the price of Widgets Inc. stock is topping out.*

Total Quality Management (TQM) (TO-tel KWAL-ih-te MAN-ej-ment): Fourteen-point approach to improving quality that was developed by Edward Deming.

> *Widgets Inc. is instituting a policy of TQM in order to get back its reputation as the maker of the best widgets in the world.*

track record (trak REK-urd): What has happened before.

My employees have a track record with me, and I have a track record with my customers.

tract (trakt): A piece of land.

George wants to develop a subdivision on the tract that he inherited from his grandfather.

trade barrier (trade BAIR-re-er): Something that blocks one country's ability to trade with another.

The biggest trade barrier the U.S. faces in trying to get its products sold on the island nation of Paradise is the high tariffs.

trademark (TRADE-mark): A logo or symbol that a maker of goods puts on a product to distinguish it from others.

The trademark of Widgets Inc., the purple widget, is recognized around the world.

trade publication (trade pub-lih-KA-shun): A magazine that is geared toward a specific business or profession.

Widgetworld magazine is a trade publication of the widget industry.

trade secret (trade SE-kret): A formula or business practice that helps a company but is only known to a few people in the company.

One night at the widget convention in Las Vegas, Randy started shooting his mouth off and gave out a trade secret about the special kinds of rubber bands that Widgets Inc. uses.

transcribe (TRAN-skribe): Writing down a number from one financial record to another.

Terence has a job transcribing numbering into the general ledger.

transfer price (trans-FER prise): A charge made within a company when one division makes something for use in another division.

The manager of our division could not believe the high transfer price charged for a machine made by R&D.

treasury note (TREZH-ure-e note): Risk-free intermediate government obligations between $1,000 and $1 million.

My bank is heavily invested in treasury notes.

trend analysis (trend ah-NAL-ih-sis): Examination of how a company performs financially over a period of time.

When Widgets Inc. did a trend analysis of the business, it learned that more widgets sell in the summer than at any other time of year.

trickle down (TRIH-kl down): Economic theory that holds that if the richest people in the country are doing well, their good fortune will inevitably trickle down to people who work for them.

Edgar Widget believes in the trickle-down theory. In fact, he said for every five million dollars extra he earns this year, he will increase his employees' pay by five cents an hour.

True North (tru north): An unyielding spot. The ultimate goal.

The president of Widgets Inc. said the company should not get caught up in tangential issues and instead should focus on True North, making better widgets.

trustee (TRUST-ee): A person who is in charge of a piece of property for another person.

After Harold's mother became sick, he was appointed trustee of her holdings.

Truth in Lending Act (truthe in LEND-ing akt): A federal law that requires lenders to disclose specific information about a loan so that a consumer can make an educated decision. It also gives a borrower three days to back out of a deal.

> *The bank has to tell you how much you will have paid for a $70,000 mortgage when it is paid off in thirty years. It has to tell you this because of the Truth in Lending Act.*

turnaround (TURN-ah-ROUND): Taking a company that is in terrible straits and making drastic changes to make it profitable again.

> *Gary is a turnaround specialist who comes into troubled companies, guts them, and makes them profitable again.*

turnkey (TURN-ke): A project that is turned over in finished form for the user of the project. The idea is that all the user has to do is turn a key and get started.

> *The new computer system at Widgets Inc. is a turnkey operation.*

turnover (TURN-O-ver): The percentage of employees who leave a company and must be replaced within a given time period.

> *Widgets Inc. has a high turnover. Employees say it is because wages are low and the stress of widget building is so high.*

umbrella policy (um-BREL-ah PO-lih-se): Insurance policy that gives extra liability coverage to an existing standard policy.

> *Widgets Inc. has an umbrella policy covering it against suits such as the one recently filed by the consumer's group.*

unaffiliated union (un-af-FIL-e-ate-ed UNE-yun): A union that is not connected with the AFL-CIO.

> *The Widget Makers Union of America is an unaffiliated union, and so is the Teamsters.*

unavoidable costs (un-ah-VOID-ah-bl kosts): Costs that a company will have regardless of company decisions about specific product lines.

> *Utility bills are unavoidable costs, as are interest payments.*

underground economy (UN-der-ground e-KON-o-me): The part of the economy that is not taxed. Most of the underground economy is illegal activity, although some would be legal if it was reported.

> *Randy is dealing in black-market widgets. Actually, Randy deals in many aspects of the underground economy.*

under the counter (UN-der the COUNT-er): Illegal payments for merchandise or service.

> *A representative of Widgets Inc. came in my store and offered me an under-the-counter payment to keep all other brands of widgets off the shelves.*

undervalued (un-der-VAL-ude): A security selling below what analysts believe is its market value.

> *Analysts believe that Stuff Company was undervalued until Widgets Inc. started trying to take it over.*

underwriter (UN-der-rite-er): The person who takes the risk of a new issue of stock by purchasing it and then attempting to resell it.

> *Thomas is the underwriter of the new issue of Widgets Inc. stock.*

unearned income (un-ERND IN-kum): Income that does not come from compensation from a job. It includes dividend and interest income.

> *My dividend payments from Widgets Inc. qualifies as unearned income.*

unemployable (un-em-PLOY-ah-bl): The people who lack basic skills and education and do not have a reasonable chance of getting or keeping a job.

> *The president of Widgets Inc. told a group of business leaders that the city's homeless problem is so bad because many of the homeless are unemployable.*

unfair competition (un-FAIR kom-peh-TISH-un): Representing one product as another to try to capitalize on the popularity of a product.

> *Widgets Inc. has been charged with unfair competition because it put its low-grade widget in a box almost identical to that of the box for the Gizmos Inc. High-Tech Widget.*

unfair labor practice (un-FAIR LA-bur PRAK-tis): Illegal practice by either management or a union.

> *The management of Widgets Inc. has been charged with an unfair labor practice for forcing employees to work holidays at straight time.*

unfavorable balance of trade (un-FA-VUR-ah-bl BAL-ens of trade): When the value of imports into a country is greater than the value of its exports.

> *The U.S. has an unfavorable balance of trade with the island country of Paradise. The only product that country imports is Elvis memorabilia, but it exports a rare plant species that is used in the wildly popular diet pill, Loseit.*

union (UNE-yun): An organized group of employees that looks out for the welfare of employees and is responsible for negotiating for employees.

> *On John's nineteenth birthday, he joined the Widget Workers of America. His father had been a member of that union for twenty-five years.*

union shop (UNE-yun shop): A shop that requires all employees to be a member of a union.

> *Harold applied for a job at Stuff Company. When he got the job, he had to join the Widget Makers Union of America, because Stuff Company is a union shop.*

UNIX (U-nix): A multi-user operating system that was designed by Bell Laboratories.

> *Carol is knowledgeable about how to program for UNIX.*

universal product code (UPC) (u pe se): A code represented by numbers and by a bar code that is used to identify a product.

> *Just scan the UPC and you will see the price of that new high-tech widget.*

unloading (un-LODE-ing): Selling off stocks and bonds while prices are declining, in an attempt to cut losses.

> *Edgar Widget is unloading all of his stock in Widgets Inc. His brother, Ernest Widget, is going to ride out the market and hopes the company their father founded comes back.*

unskilled (un-SKILD): A worker who has no special skills or talents.

> *Everyone knows that widget making is a complex process. Widgets Inc. will not hire unskilled workers for anything except janitorial duties.*

up front (up-FRONT): Money that is given as soon as there is an agreement.

> *Smartypants Software received $10,000 up front for the widget-making software. When the project is finished, Smartypants Software will receive another $10,000.*

upload (UP-lode): Sending data from a computer to a network.

Jane is going to upload the logo of her new company into the business discussion group she found on the Internet.

uptick (UP-tik): When the price of the last trade of stock is higher than the price of the previous trade of the same stock.

George sold his stock in Widgets Inc. at the first uptick of the day.

uptime (UP-time): The time when a machine, workers, or a factory is operational.

With all the broken machines around here, this factory does not have a lot of uptime.

upwardly mobile (UP-werd-le MO-bile): A group of people who are earning significantly more than they once were.

When Ralph got promoted, his brother said, "Welcome to the ranks of the upwardly mobile."

user friendly (UZE-er FREND-le): The ease and simplicity of use of computer hardware and software.

This new accounting software by Smartypants Software is advertised as being user friendly.

utility (u-TIL-ih-te): A service that is useful to the public, especially electricity, gas, telephone, water, and sewerage services.

Our biggest expense besides rent is all of our utility bills.

utility easement (u-TIL-ih-te EZ-ment): The use of private property to run utility lines.

Bill granted the gas company a utility easement to run gas lines along his property.

vacancy rate (VA-ken-se rate): The percentage of units in a building or development that are not occupied.

> *Widgets Inc. developed a new Widget Mall in Toledo but it didn't get many tenants. In fact, the vacancy rate is higher than 50 percent.*

vacation pay (va-KA-shun pa): The compensation an employee receives while on vacation.

> *Harry was always self-employed before he went to work for Widgets Inc. This is the first time in his life that he will receive vacation pay.*

value added (VAL-u AD-ed): A way of assigning value at each stage of production. At each stage, there is the cost of materials to get to that stage and the price of the item at that stage. The difference is the value added.

> *In widget making, there is a lot of value added by production.*

variable rate mortgage (VAR-e-ah-bl rate MOR-gej): A long-term mortgage that is subject to rate adjustments every six months for the term of the loan.

> *Norman has a variable rate mortgage on his house. The last time it was adjusted, the rate went down.*

variance (VAR-e-ens): An exemption from a zoning law by a zoning authority.

> *Even though zoning in this area didn't allow a factory, the zoning board in town granted a variance and the factory is now being built.*

vendor (VEND-ur): One who sells things.

> *Alfred is a widget vendor. He sells widgets.*

venture capital (VEN-chure KAP-ih-tel): Money that is put forth by investors to fund startup companies.

Smartypants Software would have never become the huge company that it is if it weren't for the early infusion of venture capital.

vertical integration (VER-tih-kel in-teh-GRA-shun): When a company dominates every step of an industry, from the gathering of raw materials to the marketing of the final product.

Widgets Inc. is getting closer to vertical integration. It even owns a rubber band factory, a plastics factory, and a factory that makes purple paint. There are only a couple of other steps it does not dominate yet.

vest (vest): When someone qualifies for a pension, he is are vested.

Greg didn't feel it was a risk for him to go looking for a new job. He had worked at Widgets Inc. for twenty-five years and he was vested. His retirement income was safe.

vice president (vise PREZ-ih-dent): A corporate officer who has authority or some functional application.

Ursula is the vice president in charge of production for Widgets Inc.

virus (VI-rus): A program that is designed to attack a computer and destroy files.

Mildred lost her novel due to a virus that got into her computer from the Internet.

volume (VOL-ume): The total number of a specific type of security that is traded in a time period.

There was a high volume traded in Widgets Inc. last quarter. Much of the interest came from the highly touted introduction of the high-tech widget.

volume discount (VOL-ume DIS-count): A discount in price given for orders of larger quantities.

Bighugestore Company gets a tremendous volume discount because it orders thousands of widgets every month.

voucher (VOUCH-er): An official piece of paper that says someone should be paid.

Every Tuesday morning, Rick turned in his pay voucher.

wage (waje): Compensation given for work.

Widget making isn't fun but it pays a decent wage.

wage ceiling (waje SELE-ing): The highest wage that someone within a wage category can receive.

Even though Elliot was the best widget maker in the company, he felt he had to pursue a better-paying job because he had reached his wage ceiling as a widget maker.

wage scale (waje skale): An outline of the rates that people get paid, for specific jobs within a company.

The reason I want to be a widget maker instead of a rubber bander is simple. Just look at the wage scale. Widget makers get paid more money.

Wall Street (wall street): An investment community commonly associated with the activities on one street in Manhattan.

Wall Street sure loves what Widgets Inc. is doing with its new high-tech widget.

warranty (war-ren-te): A written guarantee that a product or service will be satisfactory or, in the event that it is not, that some sort of recompence, such as a refund or a repair, will be performed. A warranty is usually only effective for a limited period of time.

Widgets Inc. widgets come with a six-year warranty.

wear and tear (wair and tair): Slow physical decay of a product from use and age.

When Stuart brought his old widget for repairs, the technician said, "This is what happens to these widgets from wear and tear."

widget (WIDJ-et): A fictional production item used as an example.

Widgets Inc. makes widgets.

wildcat strike (WILD-kat strike): Illegal, sudden strike by rank-and-file employees without the approval of union leadership.

When the dispute with Widgets Inc. and the union went nowhere, the workers on the left-handed widget maker press went on a wildcat strike to demand safer conditions on that press.

window of opportunity (WIN-do of op-pur-TU-nih-te): The time period when a person or company has a chance to make something happen.

My Dad told me to always be ready because I would never know when I would get a window of opportunity.

Windows (WIN-doze): A Microsoft operating system that gives the user an easy-to-use, symbolic graphical interface.

My eight-year-old son taught me how to use Windows.

withholding (with-HOLDE-ing): The part of an employee's wages that are not given to the employee but are instead used for taxes, health benefits, union dues, and other items.

When Alan examined his paycheck, he realized a lot was deducted in withholding.

workers compensation (WERK-ers kom-pen-SA-shun): Payment made by a company, or the insurance company of a company, that employed a person who was hurt on the job.

Randall was hurt on the widget press five years ago and he has been collecting workers compensation ever since.

work order (WERK OR-der): A request for work from one department in a company to another.

> *The head of the marketing department put in a work order for 1,000 special green widgets for St. Patrick's Day.*

work station (werk STA-shun): A place specifically set up for one person to work.

> *It is against Widgets Inc. policy to put up a picture of your family in your work station. The only decorative piece allowed is one of five Widgets Inc. logos.*

Yankee bonds (YANG-kee bonds): Bonds that foreign investors sell in America, in American currency, mostly to Americans.

> *Trudy bought Yankee bonds because it gave her familiarity with the currency and some exotic intrigue as well.*

year to date (year to date): How much an account has accumulated since the first of the year.

> *Our sales this year to date are tremendous.*

yield (yeeld): A return on investment.

> *My uncle Elmer told me the yield on Widgets Inc. stock hasn't fallen below 20 percent in fifty years.*

yuppie (YUP-pe): Young Urban Professional. The acronym yuppie is an often derisive term implying greedy, selfish, arrogant, shallow urban professionals.

> *Victoria says she is not a yuppie. "It's only a coincidence that I drive a four-wheel drive vehicle onto my cul-de-sac, while carrying imported cheese and ingredients for my pasta-making machine that my au-pair should have shined today with my son, Ulysses."*

zero-based budgeting (ZE-ro based BUDJ-et-ing): A way of budgeting in which every dollar must be justified, not just every new dollar. In other words, all money requested is examined, instead of just money requested that is higher than a previous budget.

> *"Widgets Inc. has instituted zero-based budgeting, meaning we have to justify almost every postage stamp," complained Smithers.*

zero-sum game (ZE-ro sum game): In such an activity, gains by one party are exactly equal to losses by another. One cannot win without someone else losing.

> *"Toughen up," yelled the manager at the apprentice widget maker. "This is a tough business. Don't worry about Winston. This is a zero-sum game. You won. But you better get to work because it doesn't end. There is always somebody else coming along and this remains a zero-sum game."*

zoning (ZONE-ing): Rules on how land can be developed.

> *Widgets Inc. wants to build a new factory in Plainville, but first the company needs the town to change the zoning to industrial.*